Pearson
PUBLISHING

Student Handbook for
English

James Durran and Jim Stewart

James Durran is Head of English at Parkside Community College in Cambridge.
Jim Stewart is Head of English at St Peter's School in Huntingdon.

Cartoons by Steve Clarke

English

Name...

Class ....

School..

....

....

Further copies of this publication may be obtained from:

Pearson Publishing
Chesterton Mill, French's Road, Cambridge CB4 3NP
Tel 01223 350555   Fax 01223 356484

Email info@pearson.co.uk   Web site http://www.pearson.co.uk/education/

ISBN: 1 85749 585 3

Published by Pearson Publishing 2000
© Pearson Publishing 2000
Revised 2000

Contents

Okay, I'm listening… give it your best shot

Introduction

This handbook will help you to:

- work confidently on your own
- produce the best work that you can.

It is designed to support work that you do in English lessons and tasks that you do at home, with advice on effective thinking, reading and writing.

The handbook contains the following features:

- a 'toolkit' for each of the main kinds of **reading** and **writing** that you will come across in English. For example, if you are making the front page of a newspaper, you will find a diagram to help you make the layout realistic. To help you  write the news reports, you will find labelled examples to show you how they have been written. If you are writing about a poem, you will find questions to ask yourself, phrases to help with expressing ideas, and reminders about how to quote. Many of the sections contain trigger phrases or words, to help you start sentences or to give you a sense of how you might write. You will need to choose and adapt these to fit the work that you are doing
- checklists to help you **edit and redraft** work
- reminders about **punctuation**
- help with preparing and giving a **formal presentation**
- explanations of **technical terms** that you will come across in English. Where these words are used in the book, they are normally in bold type.

1 Toolkits for Reading

Reading any text

The following are some basic questions to ask about any text – whether it is a poem, a film, a television programme, a picture, a novel, or an advertisement:

What form of text is it?

◆ Is it a text that you read on a page, look at on a screen, or listen to?

◆ Is it mainly images, mainly words or a mixture of both? If it contains images, are these moving or still?

What genre of text is it?

◆ For example, if it is a television programme, what kind is it? Is it a comedy, a documentary, a news programme, a drama, a soap opera...

◆ Does it fit into a sub-genre? For example, if it is a drama, is it a police drama, a hospital drama, or another kind? What makes it fit into this sub-genre? What rules does it follow?

Who made the text?

- Was it one person, or more than one?
- What do you know about them, or what can you work out?
- Does knowing this make a difference to the way you read the text?

Who has given you the text, or allowed you to read it?

- Is it a teacher, a television channel, a magazine publisher, the Internet?
- Does knowing this affect the way you read the text?

What is the purpose of the text?

- Is it to persuade, to explore, to inform, to explain, to entertain, to instruct...?
- How has it been made to do this?
- How successful is it?

What is the audience for the text?

- Who is meant to read, view or hear it? How do you know? How is it aimed at them?
- How might different readers read the text differently?
- How does being the person you are affect the way you read the text?

Quoting from texts

If you are writing about a text, it is important to quote words and phrases as evidence for your ideas.

This example of quoting from a poem shows how to set out quotations. The most important thing is to make it very clear which words are quoted and which words are your own:

> Set longer quotations in from the margins, leaving a blank line above and below

> Single inverted commas round titles of poems or stories (underline titles of whole books)

The opening lines of 'The Send-Off' immediately create a sense of mixed, strong emotions:

> "Down close, darkening lanes they sang their way
> To the siding shed,
> And lined the train with faces grimly gay."

Words such as "darkening", "close" and "grimly" give a sense of foreboding, contrasting with the description of how the soldiers "sang their way". This contradiction is summed up in the oxymoron "faces grimly gay".

> Keep quotations short – two or three lines will usually be enough

> In a list of quoted words, each one has its own quotation marks

> If possible, weave brief quotations into your own sentences

Reading for information or ideas

In English, you may need to look in texts for facts and opinions. For example, you may be writing a report on a subject, or a guide to a place. You may be going to take part in a debate on an issue, or you might be organising a visit. You might be making a poster on a topic, or finding out about the place where you will be doing your work experience.

The instructions were simple…
But so (too) was the builder!

Where to look

You might look for information in any of the following:

- newspaper reports
- encyclopaedias
- Web pages
- textbooks
- magazine articles
- CD-ROMs
- leaflets
- teletext.

Skimming and scanning the text

This kind of reading is not about reading individual words, one after the other. It is about looking at large chunks of text, and spotting particular words or ideas in them. This involves moving your eye quickly down the page, resting at three or four points, and looking for key words or phrases. This is a very useful skill and worth practising.

Annotating

Annotation is helpful for noting:

- ◆ key words
- ◆ relevant opinions
- ◆ relevant facts
- ◆ useful quotations.

The article below is about a new theme park, and is biased in favour of it. It has been annotated by a student who is looking for arguments against the park for a debate:

We will transform local park, vows company

by Paula Reeves

LARK MEADOW COUNTRY PARK is set to be transformed, if plans for a new theme park are given the go-ahead by local councillors.

money going out of local community

American company Theme Parks Inc. have submitted plans for developing the park over the next two years.

Hope

Roads already crowded

"We hope that people will come from all over the region to enjoy this major new attraction," said TPI's Public Relations Manager, Nicola Perkins.

"This is a fantastic opportunity for employment in Larkdale, and will give pleasure to hundreds of thousands of people every year."

Important
(find out more)

Only small

Wildlife reduced

Healthy activities

Paying for what is
currently free

Downgrading of jobs

Bound to be affected

Reassured

Local environmental campaigners have <u>expressed concern</u> at the proposal.

However, Ms Perkins reassured reporters that there would be a <u>small conservation area</u> at the park in which visitors would be able to see <u>some of the animals and plants</u> which currently live in the woods and rough ground.

"People who <u>used to walk and cycle</u> in the park will now be able to enjoy new leisure opportunities, at a <u>very reasonable cost.</u>"

Wildlife

She also gave an assurance that the wildlife wardens currently employed would be offered jobs in the new park.

"We will need ride attendants, and people to sell food and souvenirs," said Ms Perkins.

Happy

Concerns that <u>Lark Meadow School</u> and the <u>nearby hospital</u> will be affected were brushed aside by Ms Perkins.

"I'm sure that the school will be happy to have the theme park nearby, and that patients at the hospital will not find the noise too inconvenient," she said.

Reading a poem

In English, you will read, talk and write about poems in a range of ways. This section is about one of them. It suggests how you might:

◆ *think analytically about poems*

◆ *organise your thoughts into writing.*

(There are more detailed questions on pages 10 and 11 to help you look at poems in more depth.)

? **Think about the title of the poem.** What does it make you think about?

The title of the poem, "...", makes me think of...

? **What did you feel and think when you first read the poem?**

When I first read the poem, I thought/wondered/imagined/felt/didn't understand/liked...

? **How does the poem begin?** What does the beginning make you feel, or imagine?

The opening words of the poem, "...", make me imagine...

? **What is the poem about?** Does it describe something? Does it tell a story? Does it have a message?

The poem is about...
It describes...
It makes me think about...
When I read the poem, I realised...

? **How is the poem divided up?** Is it in **stanzas**? Are there different sections? Why do you think the poet has done this?

The poem is divided into...
This helps to...

❓ **Does the poem have a particular mood or atmosphere?** What words or phrases create this mood?

Words such as "..." and "..." create a mood of...

❓ **Look for these in the poem:**
- metaphors
- similes
- alliteration
- onomatopoeia
- personification.

How do they help the writer to describe places, feelings, people and so on?

The... is described as a... This makes it seem... The poet uses lots of "s" sounds to... The sound of the word "..." helps you to hear the... ... is personified as a...

❓ **Pick out some important words from the poem.** What do they make you feel, or think about, or imagine?

The word "..." reminds me of... It makes the... seem...

❓ **What do you think is the most important line in the poem? Why?**

I think the most important line is... because...

❓ **What lines or images in the poem do you think are most effective? Why?**

The image that I found most effective was... because it reminded me of...

❓ **What do you like or not like about the poem?**

I liked the way the poem... I didn't understand...

Reading a poem in more depth

The following questions will help you to analyse a poem in depth. You might choose some of them, or try to answer them all.

Deep down the poem was far
more interesting...

❓ **Think about the title of the poem.** What does it lead you to expect? (You could think about this before you read, and then again later.)

The title suggests...
It refers to...

❓ **What did you feel and think when you first read the poem?**

When I first read the poem, I thought/wondered/imagined/ felt/didn't understand/liked...

❓ **What can you say about the way the poem begins, and the way it ends?**

The opening words of the poem, "...", create a sense of...
The poem ends on a note of...

❓ **Can you sum up briefly what the poem is about?** Is it describing a place, or an experience, or a person? Is it telling a story? Is it asking questions? Is it exploring ideas?

The poem is about...
It raises the idea of... making me think about...

❓ What can you say about the form of the poem? What can you say about the length of the lines, the use of **rhythm**, the use of rhyme, the way the **stanzas** or verses are divided up? How do these things relate to the meaning of the poem? How do they affect the way you read it? Does the poem have a particular form – a haiku, or a **sonnet**, for example? Look for any patterns in the poem: why are they there?

The idea of... is reflected in the rhythm, which...
The rhyming of "..." and "..." emphasises...
The regular rhymes create a feeling of...
This poem is an example of a...

❓ What can you say about the pace of the poem?

The poem moves...
The rhythm creates a... pace which...
The pace changes when...

❓ Does the poem seem to have a particular mood or tone? How do particular words and phrases help to create this **mood**? What emotions does the poem suggest to you? How are they expressed?

Words such as "..." and "..." create a mood of...
The image of "..." conveys a feeling of...

❓ What is the voice behind the poem? Does it seem to be the poet, or is it a character he/she has created? What do they seem to be like? What makes you feel this?

The poem is written from the point of view of...
Phrases such as "..." and "..." make the poet seem...

? **What can you say about the language of the poem?** Is it simple and direct; is it complicated? Why do think the poet has chosen to write in this way? Which devices does the poet use – **metaphors, similes, alliteration, onomatopoeia, symbolism, personification** and so on? Which individual words or phrases could you explore in detail? What feelings or ideas do they suggest?

The poem's language is...
Words such as "..." have the effect of...
The metaphor of "..." is effective because...
The poet uses... to describe the...
The alliteration in the line "..." imitates the...
The repeated "s" sounds in... create a feeling of...
... is personified as...
... symbolises...

? **How might different readers read the poem differently?** How does being the person you are, living in the time and place you do, make you read the poem?

When it was written, readers would have understood that...
A reader today, however...
The poem reflects the poet's culture by...

? **What do you think is the overall effect of the poem? Can it be read on more than one level?** What do you think the poet is saying? Does the poem have a message or a moral? Is **symbolism** important? How?

At a deeper level, the poem is about...
... is a symbol for...
The poem seems to be saying...
The poem can be read as...
I think the poet wants the reader to feel/understand/ think about/explore/imagine/ question/look again at...

Reading a short story

In English, you will read, talk and write about stories in a range of ways. This section is about one of them – thinking about how a story is written.

...So, now are you sitting comfortably?

❓ **What did you feel and think when you first read the story?**

When I first read the story, I thought/felt/ wondered/imagined/didn't understand/liked...

❓ **Think about the title of the story.** What does it lead you to expect? (You could think about this before you read, and then again later.)

The title suggests... It refers to...

❓ **What can you say about the opening words of the story?**

The opening words of the story, "...", create a sense of...

❓ **Who is telling the story?** Is it one (or more) of the characters? Is it someone outside the story? Do we believe what they tell us? What is the effect of the story being told in this way?

Because the story is told by..., the reader needs to remember that...

? **What can you say about the structure of the story?** Does it have a clear beginning and a definite ending? How is the situation established at the beginning of the story? How has it changed by the end? Is there a turning point?

At the beginning of the story...
However, by the end...
The turning point is when...
The effect of this is...

? **What can you say about the main character(s)?** (See also page 16.) What do you learn about them, and how? How do you feel about them? How do they speak, and how does this reflect their character? How have they changed by the end of the story, and why?

The main character(s) is/are...
The way that... speaks, shows... For example...
By the end of the story...
The writer describes... as "...", which makes me think...

? **From whose viewpoint is the story told?**

We see the events of the story from the point of view of...
We learn most about the thoughts and feelings of...
This has the effect of...

? **What can you say about the mood of the story?** How do particular words and phrases help to create this **mood**? What emotions does the story suggest to you? How are they expressed?

Words such as "..." and "..." create a mood of...
The image of "..." conveys a feeling of...
The mood changes when...

What can you say about the language of the story? Is it simple and direct; is it complicated? How formal is the language? Does it contain **slang** or **dialect**? How does the language of the story reflect the time in which it was written?

The writer uses language which is...
Words such as "..." reflect...
The use of dialect in the story emphasises...

How might different readers read the story differently? How does being the person you are, living in the time and place you do, make you read it?

When it was written, readers would have understood that...
A reader today, however...
The story reflects the writer's culture by...

Can the story be read on more than one level? Does the story have a message, or a moral? Is **symbolism** important? How? Is the story a **fable** or an **allegory**?

The story seems to be saying that...
At a deeper level, the story is about...
... is a symbol for...
Each character represents an aspect of...

He needed to be sure that the story worked on different levels...

Reading a character

These questions will help you if you are thinking, talking or writing about a character in detail. You might choose some of them, or try to answer them all. (If you are writing in role as a character, see page 52.)

You're not quite what I had in mind for Romeo...

? **Can you sum up the character using a few adjectives?**

I would describe this character as...

? **How does the character relate to other characters?**

... is liked/not liked/feared/admired (etc) by...
... is more/less powerful than... because...
... treats other characters in a... way, for example...

? **How does the character feel or think about events in the story?**

When... happens, ... seems to feel...

? **Is the appearance of the character important?** Does the way they look or dress reflect their personality?

... is described as...
This makes them seem...
They wear..., which reflects...

❓ **Look at verbs connected with the character.** What do these tell you about them?

Verbs such as "..." and "..." make this character seem...
The writer uses words such as "..." and "..." to describe the way... moves/ speaks/looks.
This reflects...

❓ **How does the narrator seem to feel about this character?** How do you think they want you – the reader – to feel about them?

I think the narrator wants the reader to feel... by...

❓ **Does the character change? If so, how?**

To start with, ... seems...
However..., by the end...
The turning point is when...

❓ **Can you sum up your own feelings about the character?**

To start with I...
However, by the end...

❓ **Can you explain the function of the character in the story, or play?** Do they represent a way of thinking, or a particular type of person, for example?

I think the character represents
This character is important because...
In the play/story/novel as a whole, this character...
This character symbolises...

Reading a persuasive text

This section will help
you to analyse a piece
of persuasive writing.
This might be a letter,
an article, an advert, a
poster, a leaflet, or
a speech.

❓ Audience and purpose
Who is the **text** aimed at?
What is it trying to make
them think, feel or believe?

*The text is aimed at...
It is aiming to make its
readers agree that...*

❓ Techniques
Look at the text to see
whether it uses any of
these techniques:

- **asserting** that
  something is the case

The writer asserts that...

- using **emotive
  language**, to arouse
  the reader's feelings

*Words such as "..." and
"..." are used to make the
reader feel...*

- providing and
  explaining **facts** or
  evidence, to support
  an argument

*The writer supports their
case by....*

- giving reasons why the reader should agree with the writer

  The writer tries to make the reader agree that... by writing that...

- using statistics to support the writer's view and to give it authority

  The writer uses the figure of... to support their argument that...

- clearly stating **opinions**

  The writer's opinion is clear when he/she writes that...

- repeating words or phrases, to emphasise ideas and points

  The repetition of... has the effect of...

- asking **rhetorical questions**

  The writer asks "..."

- writing in a strong **voice** to emphasise a point

  The writer emphasises the point that... by writing "..."

- appealing to the reader directly.

  The writer tells the reader directly "..."

Structure
What can you say about the **structure**? How does the text begin? How does the writer develop the argument? How does the text end?

*The writer begins by...
This is followed by...
The argument is developed by...
The text ends with...*

Reading an advertisement

The questions below will help you to think, talk and write about an advertisement. The sections Reading a persuasive text (page 18) and Reading an image (page 29) will help you to analyse advertisements in more detail.

? **What is being advertised?**

This is an advert for...

? **Where would you find this advert?**

This advert is from...
You would expect to find this advert...

? **What kind of advert is it? Does it remind you of others?**

It is typical of...
It reminds me of...

? **Who is the advert aimed at?** What type of person? What age? What gender? How can you tell?

The target audience is...
They would probably be...
This is clear from...

? **What is it saying about the product?** What does it connect the product with? What does it say the product can do for the buyer?

The advert is saying...
It connects the product with...
... suggests that...
It gives the impression that... by...
It implies ...
The viewer/reader is meant to feel...
The product is made to seem...

How does it do this? What does the image (or images) show about the product? How does the advert use words to give a message about the product? Does it tell a story? How? Does it create a particular mood? How? What does it show people doing, saying or feeling?

The image shows...
Details such as... suggest...
Words such as "..." and "..." give a sense of...
The story of... is told by...
The advert creates a mood of... by..., which makes the product seem...
The advert shows people...
This suggests that...

How does the advert make different groups of people seem – children, adults, women, men...? Does it do this in a fair way? Does it **stereotype** people?

The advert represents... as being...
This seems an unfair way of showing...
... are stereotyped as...

These key words might help you to think about and comment on any advert. They are all explained in *Chapter 6: Technical Terms* (page 100):

- audience
- alliteration
- ambiguity
- assertion
- emotive language
- genre
- homophone
- imagery
- imperative
- layout
- logo
- mood
- narrative
- persuasive language
- pun
- representation
- rhetorical question
- slogan
- stereotype
- symbol
- tone
- viewpoint

Reading a newspaper report

These questions will help you to read, discuss or write in depth about how a newspaper report has been written.

❓ **What can you say about the headline?** What does it lead you to expect? What can you say about the language that it uses? What effect is it meant to have?

This headline suggests that the report will be...
It is meant to make the reader feel...
The words "..." and "..." suggest...

❓ **If there are any photographs, what are their effects?** How do they make people seem? How might they make the reader feel? What can you say about the captions? Do they encourage a particular reading of the photographs?

The photograph makes... seem... and...
The caption "..." leads the reader to look for...

❓ **How much of the report is fact, and how much is opinion?** Can you say anything about what information has been included, and what has been left out? Can you work out the writer's **opinion** about the subject? How?

The writer has used information which makes... seem..., such as...
There are no facts to suggest...

Are the opinions of particular people being put across more strongly than others?	*The writer seems to believe that...* *This is made clear by...*
Does the report contain emotive language? Are there any words and phrases (in the **headline**, report, subheads, crossheads, etc), which might stir up the reader's emotions? How are they part of the overall effect of the report?	*The reader is encouraged to feel..., by words such as " ... " and " ... "* *Words such as " ... " and " ... " make... seem...* *This adds to the overall sense that...*
What can you say about the way the report starts and ends?	*The first sentence creates the feeling that...* *The report concludes with a...*
What can you say about how the report has been presented on the page? How does this affect the way you read the story? Think about the size of the **headline**, the size and positioning of the picture, any crossheads, and the use of italics, capital letters and bold type to emphasise parts of the story.	*The headline is... and... which makes it seem...* *The photographs are placed so that...* *Italics and bold print are used to emphasise..., so that...* *The overall effect of the layout on the reader is...*

? **What else can you say about the language of the report?** Has the writer used **alliteration**, **metaphors** or **similes**, for example?

The writer describes the... as...
The effect of this is...
The writer uses... to create a sense of...

? **How are different people represented (made to seem) in the report?** How are they described? How much importance are they given in the report? (What is their status?) Are they named? How much of the report is given to what they have to say? Where in the report does this come?

... is represented as...
... is described as "...",
which suggests that...
... is given more status than..., because...

It is often helpful to annotate the report, highlighting its main features, to help you to talk or write about it. The following example shows how you might do this:

Positive, supportive headline

We will transform local park, vows company

by Paula Reeves

Positive language (underlined throughout)

LARK MEADOW COUNTRY PARK is set to <u>be transformed</u>, if plans for a new theme park are given the go-ahead by local councillors.

American company Theme Parks Inc. have submitted plans for <u>developing</u> the park over the next two years.

Given lots of space.
Quoted at length.
Her opinions are
not challenged.

Hope

"We hope that people will come from all over the region to <u>enjoy</u> this <u>major new attraction</u>," said TPI's <u>Public</u> Relations Manager, Nicola Perkins.

"This is a <u>fantastic opportunity</u> for <u>employment</u> in Larkdale, and will give <u>pleasure</u> to <u>hundreds of thousands</u> of people every year."

Reassured

Not named
Not quoted

Local environmental campaigners have expressed concern at the proposal.

Bad things are
treated lightly

However, Ms Perkins <u>reassured</u> reporters that there would be a small conservation area at the park in which visitors would be able to see some of the animals and plants which currently live in the woods and rough ground.

"People who used to walk and cycle in the park will now be able to enjoy new leisure <u>opportunities</u>, at a very <u>reasonable</u> cost."

Wildlife

She also gave an <u>assurance</u> that the wildlife wardens currently employed would be offered jobs in the new park.

Not challenged

"We will need ride attendants, and people to sell food and souvenirs," said Ms Perkins.

Strong, supportive
crossheads

Happy

Each concern is
answered with a
quotation (structure)

Concerns that Lark Meadow School and the nearby hospital will be affected were brushed aside by Ms Perkins.

Assertion

(Nicola Perkins given
the last word)

"I'm sure that the school will be <u>happy</u> to have the theme park nearby, and that patients at the hospital will not find the noise too inconvenient," she said.

Keeping a reading journal

You may be asked to record your thoughts and feelings about a novel or play that you are reading in class or on your own in the form of a journal.

Purpose

A journal is an effective way to organise your thoughts and feelings about what you are reading, by putting them into words. It also gives you a useful record of how your thoughts have developed as you read.

Audience

The **audience** will probably be yourself, so you can write informally, in a way that you will be able easily to understand.

Ideas for writing

The following questions will help you to think of what to write. (Do not just work through them in order; think about which ones you can answer in interesting ways.)

? **Have your feelings about the text changed?**

When I started reading I felt... but...

? **Have you any questions about the story, about the characters, or about the way the text has been written?**

I wonder why the writer has...
Why does...?
What will...?

?   **Have you noticed anything interesting about the way the text, or a part of the text, has been written?**

The writer has used...
The way the story is written changes, because...

?   **What questions would you ask the writer at this point?**

I would ask the writer why...

?   **What do you think is going to happen next, or later in the text? Why?**

I think there will be...
I'm sure that when...

?   **What are the characters like?** Have you found out anything new about them?

The character... is...
I now know that...

?   **What do you feel about the characters? Why?**

I feel... because...

?   **Have you any questions you would like to ask a character?**

I would ask... why he/she...

?   **What would you do next if you were one of the characters?**

If I was..., I would...

?   **Is there a part of the text that you have particularly enjoyed?**

I have most enjoyed... because...

? **Does the story, or a character, remind you of your own experiences in any way?**

... reminds me of when...

? **Does the text remind you of anything else you have read?**

... reminded me of the story /film /play...

Reading an image

The following questions will help you to read, discuss or write about a visual image, such as a photograph, an advert or a still from a film.

Instinctively, he adopted the 'expert's view'

Personal response

❓ What effect does the image have on you? Does it make you feel something, remind you of anything, see something in a particular way?

This image makes me think / feel / wonder...
To me, this image seems...

Starting to analyse the image

❓ What can you see in the image?

This image shows...

❓ Look at any people in the image – their postures, expressions and clothing. How are they made to seem here? For example, are they made to look powerful or weak? Is the viewer meant to feel sympathy for them, or not? Are they being shown in a **stereotypical** way, or as individuals? How do they relate to each other?

... is made to seem...
Details such as... may make the viewer feel...

? **Look at details in the image.** What feelings or ideas could they suggest? Do they remind you of other images? Are they **symbolic** in any way?

A sense of... is built up by...
... may remind the viewer of...
... is symbolic of...

Questions to help you look more closely at an image

? **What is the viewer's eye drawn to?** How does this affect the way the viewer might read the image?

Because of... the viewer's eye is drawn to...

? **What sort of lines is the viewer's eye drawn along?** These might be lines of action or the direction a character is looking.

The viewer's eye moves between... and...
This makes the viewer think about...

? **What is in the background, and what is in the foreground?** What do you think are the reasons for this?

The background shows...
Having... in the foreground emphasises...

? **What viewpoint does the image show?** What is the effect of this?

The image shows the viewpoint of...
This helps the viewer to feel...

Other questions to consider, if the image is a photograph or from a film

? **What can you say about the camera work?** Think about camera distance and angle, and about where the camera has been placed.

The camera is positioned...
This creates a sense of...

❓ **What can you say about the way the shot has been lit?** What are the effects of this?

... is emphasised by the lighting, which is...

More questions to consider, if the image is a still frame from a film

❓ **How is this an important image in the film?**

This is an important image in the film because...

❓ **If you have seen this part of the film, what can you say about how the camera is moving – panning, tracking or zooming; quickly or slowly; smoothly or shakily?**

The movement of the camera adds to the feeling of... by...

❓ **Does this shot remind you of other images in the film?**

This shot echoes the moment when...

The movement of the camera added to the feeling of nausea

2 Toolkits for Writing

Writing a discussion

In this kind of writing you are presenting all sides of an issue. For example, you might discuss the arguments for and against having a school uniform, or you might explore the different views people have about drugs. Usually, each point supporting one view will be followed by a point supporting the opposing view, so that there is a balanced discussion. (See opposite.)

You're ink-redible

Purpose

You are aiming to help the reader to understand different **points of view** by examining all sides of the debate. You may end by stating your own point of view, having considered others.

Audience

You may be writing for a particular **audience**. Perhaps you are explaining the issues to younger readers, or perhaps you are writing a report on a topic for a school magazine. It is important to present the ideas in a way that this audience will understand; in a way that will make them think about the issues. What will they know already? What will need explaining?

Planning

When you have collected as many different views and arguments about the topic as you can, you need to plan your piece of writing.

The example below is a plan for writing about whether experiments on live animals are acceptable. It is a paragraph plan and it also summarises the main points, which will be explored in detail:

<u>For and against animal experiments</u>

<u>Introductory paragraph</u>
"When you take a medicine, or use a cosmetic, do you know how it was tested? Well..." Why is it an important issue?
Facts about how much testing happens.

<u>Arguments on each side</u>
(include quotations, statistics and other evidence)

<u>Against</u>	<u>For</u>
Alternative research methods are available	Speeds up medical research
Unnecessary cruelty	Better that animals suffer than people
Animals and humans are so different that many results of this research are meaningless	The most reliable way to research effects of drugs is on something that is alive
Much of the testing is unnecessary (too many experiments)	Labs and experiments are controlled so that animals do not suffer unnecessarily
Lots of the research is for luxury items, such as cosmetics	People will use cosmetics, and it is essential that they are completely safe

<u>Concluding paragraph</u>
Summary – own thoughts

Useful words and phrases

Phrases to help you present two sides of a discussion include:

On the one hand...	On the other...
It could be said that...	However, it could also be said that...
One point of view is that...	Alternatively...
There is some evidence that...	Equally, there is some evidence that...
Some people feel strongly that...	Despite this...
Whereas many people feel...	...others feel...
It could be argued...	Nevertheless...

Phrases to help you present evidence include:

For example,...
Similarly...
Research shows...
This is supported by...
Statistics show that...

The truth, but not the whole truth... in fact, nothing like the truth!

Words to help you to develop points include:

Consequently,...
Therefore...
Since...
... so...
In fact...

Redrafting

- ✔ Have you introduced the topic clearly?
- ✔ Have you explained each side of the debate clearly?
- ✔ Are the points in the best order?
- ✔ Have you summarised or concluded the debate effectively at the end?

The debate was now
concluded...

Writing to explain

This section will help you to plan and write an explanation, such as a guide to a hobby or interest, a piece of writing on why language changes over time, or a talk about how to prepare for work experience.

Purpose

The purpose of an explanation is to enable someone to understand a process or idea. It might be the answer to a question. An explanation might include instructions (see page 40).

Audience

You will be writing for a particular **audience** and it is important that you keep them in mind as you write. Are you using language that your audience will understand? What do they know already? What will need more explanation?

Preparation

It might be useful to think about the following:

Information

What	...is needed?	**When**	...did you...?
	...happened?		...should you...?
	...happens next?		...does...?
	...is a...		...(etc)
	(etc)		...do you...?
			...did I...?
Where	...should you...?		...will...?
	...can you find...?		(etc)
	...did...?		
	...does...?		
	(etc)		

Explanation

How ...do/does/did...?
...should/could/might...?
...has...?
...do you...?
...did I...?
...will...?
(etc)

Why ...do/does/did...?
...should/could/might...?
...has...?

Who ...is...?
...is involved?
...does...?
...has...?
(etc)

Useful phrases for starting and joining sentences

Explaining why	... because... ... as... Consequently... Therefore... Since... ... so... As a result...
Putting ideas into order	First(ly)... Secondly... etc. Next... ... then... ... as long as... Meanwhile... Whenever... Eventually... Finally... ... after(wards)...
Developing ideas	What is more... In addition...
Giving examples	For example... ... such as... ... suggested by...

Comparing ideas and examples	Equally... Similarly... In the same way... As with... Likewise... Again... However... Although... Nevertheless... Despite this... Alternatively... On the other hand... Whereas... Compared to...
Emphasising ideas	In particular... ... more important... Significantly... Specifically... ... especially... Above all...
Concluding	In brief... On the whole... To sum up... In conclusion...

Presentation

If you are explaining something complicated, you should set out your writing in as clear a way as possible.

Can you use any of the following?

- ✔ images
- ✔ symbols
- ✔ flow diagram
- ✔ numbered points
- ✔ colour
- ✔ columns
- ✔ diagrams
- ✔ subheadings
- ✔ bullet points
- ✔ boxes
- ✔ bold, italic or underlined type.

Redrafting

- ✔ Have you set out your explanation as clearly as possible?
- ✔ Are the stages of your explanation in a logical order?
- ✔ Will your reader be able to follow your explanation easily?
- ✔ Do any technical ideas need more explaining?

Writing instructions

This section will help you to write instructions such as a recipe, or a guide to using a video camera.

Remove from heat
and stand in cold
water...

Purpose

The purpose of instructions is to tell someone how to do something.

Instructions might form part of an explanation (see page 36), such as a guide to a new hobby.

Audience

You will be writing for a particular **audience**, and it is important that you keep them in mind as you write. Are you using language that your audience will understand? Are you being too formal, or too informal? What do they know already? What will need more explanation?

Planning

Instructions will almost always be presented as a series of steps. This has to be logical and carefully planned. Plan an order for your points; they should be short and easy to follow. For example:

What will these instructions help the reader, or listener, to do?	These instructions will help you to... When you have... you will have...

What will be needed?	Before you start... You will need... Make sure that...

Take the reader (or listener) through the process, one step at a time: 1 ... 2 ... 3 ... ... and so on Each step will be a separate paragraph, or numbered point.	First of all... Secondly, look... Next, put... Now, take out... Having... you need to... You should... You could... In order to... So that... Make sure that...	Immediately... After having... Meanwhile... Whenever... When you have... Eventually... Finally... Afterwards...

Finish with some important reminders. Tell the reader (or listener) what they should have achieved.	It is important to... It is essential that... Above all... Don't forget...	You should now... You have now... You will now be able to...

Language

Instructions need to be clear and easy to follow:

- ✔ Use **imperative** verbs. For example, "Put...", "Take out...", "Pre-heat...", "Use...".
- ✔ Use short, simple **sentences**.
- ✔ Address the reader directly. For example, "You should...".

Presentation

Could you:

- ✔ number each step?
- ✔ use subheadings?
- ✔ use **bullet points**?
- ✔ use arrows (as in the diagram on page 41)?
- ✔ put key words in bold type, or underline them?
- ✔ put each step in a box?

The bullet points were simple, but effective

Instructions can also be presented visually, using diagrams, maps or pictures, for example. Think about how and where words on their own might not be clear.

Redrafting

- ✔ Have you presented the instructions on the page in a clear way?
- ✔ Are the steps in the instructions in a logical order?
- ✔ Will each step of the instructions be completely clear to your reader?
- ✔ Do any technical terms need more explanation?

Writing to persuade or to argue

This section contains reminders about how to make a piece of writing persuasive. It might be a letter, an article, an advert, a poster, a leaflet, a script for a speech, or an essay giving your view on something.

Purpose

You are trying to make your reader feel, think or do something.

Audience

You will be writing for a particular **audience**, and it is important that you keep them in mind as you write. What will persuade them?

Techniques

This is a list of techniques that you might use to make a piece of writing persuasive. The words in bold type are all explained in *Chapter 6: Technical Terms* (page 100):

✔ **assertion**
It is obvious that...

✔ **emotive language**, to arouse the reader's feelings
... terrible... charming... cruel... beautiful... appalling... abandoned... lost... little...

✔ **facts** or evidence, to support an argument
It is quite legal to... For example...

✔ **giving reasons**

If... then...
It is clear from... that...

✔ **commentary,** to explain how the facts support your point of view

Facts such as this show...

✔ statistics

In 2000, 12,000 animals were used in...

✔ clearly stated **opinions**

I believe that this is completely wrong, and...

✔ **repetition** of words or phrases, to emphasise ideas and points

These animals suffer, these animals are put through torment, and these animals die, so that our eyes won't sting if we get shampoo in them.

✔ **rhetorical questions**

Is this the behaviour we expect of a civilised society?

✔ a strong **voice**

This must end.

✔ appealing to the reader directly

You may think that...
You too can...
Next time you...

Words to start and join sentences

Listing points	First(ly)... Secondly... etc.
Giving examples	For example,... ... such as... ... as shown by...
Reasoning logically	If... then... It is clear from... that...
Adding examples or points	... also... In the same way... As with... What's more,...
Developing points	... because/as... Consequently,... Therefore... Since... In fact...
Emphasising a point	In particular,... Significantly,... Specifically,... ... especially... Above all,...
Arguing against another point of view	However... Although... Nevertheless... Despite this... On the other hand... Whereas...

DON'T **YOU** START...

Making something seem obvious

Clearly...
... of course...
Naturally...
Obviously...
Surely...
Certainly...

Concluding

On the whole...
Finally...
In conclusion...

Planning

Plan your writing carefully. Try the following series of steps:

> Start strongly – perhaps with a striking
> *fact*, or a *rhetorical question.*

> Plan a series of points, which build to
> a *concluding paragraph.*
>
> Always support opinions and ideas with
> facts, and comment on the facts
> you choose, ie:
>
> *comment/opinion*
> *fact*
> *comment/opinion*
> *fact*
> *comment/opinion*
> *(and so on)*
>
> Keep your paragraphs and sentences
> short and easy to follow. This will help
> the reader to understand your point.

End with another striking fact, or a
direct appeal to the reader, or a
strong *rhetorical question*.

Redrafting

✔ If you were the reader, how persuasive would you find
your writing?

✔ Could you be using any more of the techniques
given on pages 43 and 44?

✔ Are you using too many of the techniques, and overdoing
the persuasion?

✔ Have you started and ended in a strong way?

You will tell me if
I overdo
the persuasion...?

Writing a short story

This section will help you to plan and write a short story.

Purpose

Stories have different purposes. For example, you might want to teach a moral lesson, to scare your reader, or to explore how people might feel in a particular situation.

It was a story with an unexpected twist...

Audience

Think about who your story is for. For example, what age group will they be? How will this affect the way you write and the kind of story that it is?

Planning

These questions will help you to plan a short story:

Narrator

♦ Who is telling the story? A **narrator**? One of the characters? ("I...") More than one of the characters, at different times?

Characters

♦ Who will the main character(s) be? What will they be like?

♦ How is the reader meant to feel about each one? Identify with them? Like them? Be unsure about them? Dislike them? Feel sorry for them?

Setting

♦ Where and when will the story be set?

♦ Will you describe the setting, or will you let the reader work it out?

Viewpoint

In a story, we will usually be aware of one character's thoughts and feelings more than others'. This is the viewpoint. It may be the person telling the story, or it may be another character if the **narrator** tells us what they see, hear, feel and think. The viewpoint may change during the story.

◆ From whose point of view are we seeing what happens? Whose mind do we get inside?

Structure

Think about how you will structure the story. Try working through the following steps:

> What is the situation or set up at the start of the story?

▼

> What happens to make this situation become interesting – to complicate it in some way, so that there is a story?

▼

> How does the story develop from this point?

▼

> How does the story end? Is there a turning point? Is there a twist, or a moment of tension, or a lesson learned? Is there a resolution, or are questions left unanswered? Is there a main message or idea?

Getting started

To ensure that your story has a strong start, think about the following points:

- ◆ How will the story begin? In the middle of something? With a puzzle? With a description of a place? With a surprise, or a shock? With something strange? With the sound of a voice? In the middle of a conversation? With a description of a character? With the ending?

Techniques

Some hints:

- ✔ Effective writing is economical – it uses as few words as possible to create the best effect. As you redraft, see if you can remove any words, phrases or **sentences** that are not necessary. (See *Drafting and Redrafting*, page 78.)
- ✔ Think about the **pace** of your story – how will you keep your reader involved and interested? For example, you could speed up the pace when you describe action, and slow it down for scene-setting and descriptions.
- ✔ Make sure that it is clear who is telling the story. Only change to another **narrator** if you want to create a particular effect.
- ✔ Vary the length of your sentences. (Long sentences might help create a slow feel; short sentences are good for creating tension or excitement.)
- ✔ Interesting writing often starts and/or ends by raising questions in the reader's mind. You do not have to answer all of the questions that your story raises: don't think that you have to tie up every loose end, or explain everything away. Leave your reader with something to think about.

Useful words

These phrases might be useful for making your story flow. (Avoid using "Then...", which becomes boring.)

When... had, she...

After the...

meanwhile...

Later,...

However,...

Eventually,...

Afterwards,...

Redrafting

✔ If you were the reader, how effective would you find your writing?

✔ Is your story well-paced?

✔ Does your story have a satisfying **structure**?

✔ Have you started and ended in a strong way?

The story was flowing more than he expected...

Writing in role as a character

You may be writing as a character in a text. Often, this will be as a diary or a letter about what has happened, and how you feel.

He was beginning to understand the character

Purpose

You may be recounting what has happened and explaining your feelings and thoughts. The purpose of a diary entry would also be to explore the character's feelings and thoughts about what has happened, and to make sense of them.

In a letter, you might want to persuade somebody to help or do something, or you may just want them to understand or share what you feel.

You are trying to show:

- ✔ your understanding of what is happening in the story or play
- ✔ your understanding of how the character thinks and feels
- ✔ your understanding of the language of the character – words or phrases that are typical of them, or their **dialect**
- ✔ your understanding of issues, problems or ideas that the story is about.

Audience

The character will be writing to himself or herself, or to someone that they know well, so the language will be informal.

Structure

Think about how you will **structure** your writing. Try working through the following steps:

> ### Getting started
> You might get the reader's attention by starting with:
> * a strong feeling
> * a striking fact
> * something mysterious.
>
> If it is a letter, you will probably start by explaining why you are writing. If it is a diary, do not begin "Dear Diary", unless that really fits the character!

> ### Middle
> You will have a series of paragraphs. Each one might be about:
> * something that has happened
> * a particular feeling
> * something that you have decided to do.

> ### Ending
> You might finish with:
> * a question, to leave the reader thinking
> * a concluding thought
> * an appeal to the reader to do or understand something
> * a decision to do something.

Useful phrases

Starting **sentences** with some of these phrases will help you to get under the surface of the character as you write:

I am writing so that...
How can I...?
Why did she...?
Meanwhile, I...
Although I...
I suppose...
First of all, I felt...
I expect...
Now I feel...
I know that...   because...
I realise now...
I remember especially...
Of course,...
I hope...
When... said... I felt...
I have to...
I'm sure that...
I'm afraid that... must have meant that...
I remember saying that...
There must be...
However,...
Perhaps...
On the other hand...
Surely...
Strangely...
I wonder if...

Language

The kind of words you use will depend on what the character is like, where they are from, and whether they are from the past or not. Consider the following:

- What sort of words are typical of them?
- Are there modern words that they wouldn't know?
- Would they use **dialect**?

No, no... this guy's really cute but wherefore the hell does he have to be a Montague?!

Redrafting

- ✔ Could you add any more thoughts or feelings?
- ✔ Could you make the language more like the character's?
- ✔ Could you improve the way you begin or end?
- ✔ Have you put paragraphs in the best places?

Writing a formal letter

This section will help you to plan,
write and present a formal letter.

Purpose and audience

The purpose of a formal letter will vary. It might be to:

- ◆ **inform** the reader
- ◆ **explain** something
- ◆ **persuade** the reader to do something.
- ◆ **advise** the reader about something
- ◆ **complain** about something

A formal letter is usually written to someone who the writer does not know personally. It will usually be on a matter of business. For example, writing to an author, writing to a newspaper, applying for a job, making a complaint, requesting information, and other things…

If you are writing in role as a character, then you are also trying to show that you understand the way that character thinks, feels and uses language.

Techniques

In a formal letter, you should:

- ✔ plan the order of paragraphs carefully
- ✔ set the letter out correctly (see opposite)
- ✔ be concise (do not use more words than necessary)
- ✔ use formal connecting words (see page 58)
- ✔ be polite
- ✔ write neatly or word-process the letter.
- ✔ check that you have made all the points you need to
- ✔ check especially carefully that there are no mistakes

You should usually **not**:

- ✗ use **slang**
- ✗ use **dialect** forms
- ✗ be too emotional.

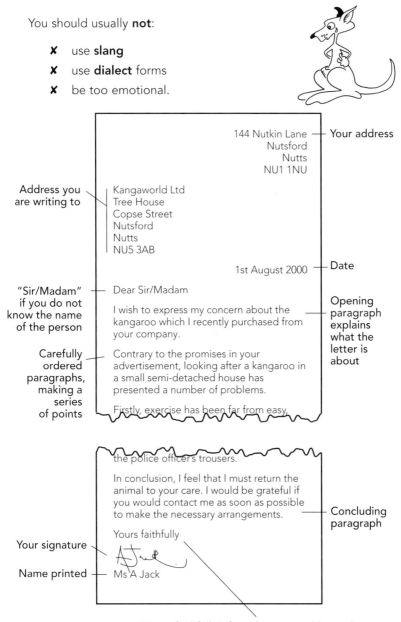

Your address — 144 Nutkin Lane
Nutsford
Nutts
NU1 1NU

Address you are writing to — Kangaworld Ltd
Tree House
Copse Street
Nutsford
Nutts
NU5 3AB

Date — 1st August 2000

"Sir/Madam" if you do not know the name of the person — Dear Sir/Madam

Opening paragraph explains what the letter is about — I wish to express my concern about the kangaroo which I recently purchased from your company.

Carefully ordered paragraphs, making a series of points — Contrary to the promises in your advertisement, looking after a kangaroo in a small semi-detached house has presented a number of problems.

Firstly, exercise has been far from easy,

the police officers' trousers.

Concluding paragraph — In conclusion, I feel that I must return the animal to your care. I would be grateful if you would contact me as soon as possible to make the necessary arrangements.

Yours faithfully

Your signature

Name printed — Ms A Jack

"Yours faithfully" if you have not addressed the person by name; "Yours sincerely" if you have addressed the person by name

The words below will help you to connect and start **sentences** in a formal style:

Firstly…	Again…	It would seem…
Secondly…etc		
Meanwhile…	However…	Obviously…
Whenever…	Although…	Evidently…
Eventually	Nevertheless…	Surely…
Finally…	Despite this…	Certainly…
	Alternatively…	…except (for)…
Consequently…	On the other hand…	Apart from…
Therefore…	On the contrary…	
Accordingly…	Whereas…	Furthermore…
Since…	Compared to…	Moreover…
Thus…		In addition…
Hence…	In particular…	
As a result…	Notably…	To sum up…
	…more important…	In conclusion…
Equally…	Significantly…	
Similarly…	Specifically…	
As with…	…especially…	
Likewise…	Above all…	
In the same way…		

Redrafting

✔ Have you thought about your **audience**, and how you need to address them?

✔ Have you written in a formal style all the way through? Have you let this slip?

✔ Are you setting the letter out properly on the page?

✔ Have you organised the letter into paragraphs?

Writing a newspaper report

This section will help you to write a newspaper report. It might be about an event from a story, or part of a media assignment, for example. The next section will help you to make a newspaper front page (see page 63).

Do you want the tabloid version or the truth?

Purpose and audience

The purpose and **audience** will depend on what type of newspaper it is. The two main types of newspaper are *tabloids* and *broadsheets*. This section will help you to write reports for both types.

Tabloid newspapers (such as *The Sun* and *The Mirror*) usually present news in a brief and easily understood way, trying to make it appeal to as many people as possible.

Broadsheet newspapers (such as *The Times* and *The Independent*) usually present the news in more detail, and have sections which comment on and analyse news events.

The purpose of a newspaper report is usually to:

- ◆ inform the reader
- ◆ recount events.

It will also always try to make the reader think or feel in a particular way, by the style in which it is written and by what is included and what is left out. (See the section on *Reading a news report*, on page 22.)

An example of a tabloid newspaper report

Tornado Terror

Strong headline

Wendy Weatherhill reports from a county literally blown away by the weather

The first paragraph should tell the reader what happened, when and where

A freak tornado ravaged the coast of Cornwall early yesterday morning.

The noise of roofs being torn off woke villagers in picturesque Mousehole soon after midnight.

Use active (not passive) verbs

Ripped

Use cross-heads to keep the reader's interest

They watched in horror as the wind ripped a path of destruction through the tourist resort.

The winds hurled objects as large as cars against buildings.

Sum up people and places with simple labels

Shopkeeper Daniel James said that he was stunned by the damage.

Choose words that encourage the reader to feel particular emotions. (Emotive language)

"We always thought our town was pretty solid, but this thing was knocking holes in stone walls!"

Include quotations from people who have been interviewed. Set these out correctly!

"It was terrifying," commented Gloucester teacher Marion Marsden, on holiday in the area.

"There was nothing anybody could do, the wind was so strong."

Keep paragraphs one sentence long

Courage

Nobody was hurt, despite the terrible conditions.

Include facts and comments that help to get across your opinions, a message or a bias. Think about how you want to represent groups of people

This was due to the courage and skill of the emergency services, who were on the scene in minutes.

"They were fantastic," commented pensioner Mrs Rhiannon Stokes.

"They knew exactly what to do, and they had us all organised."

Clearing up in the village

You could end with:
- *a quotation*
- *an opinion*
- *a new fact, which leaves a strong impression*
- *a question, to leave the reader thinking*

An example of a broadsheet newspaper report

Tornado Devastates Cornwall

by Eddie Currents

The south coast of Cornwall was struck by a violent tornado in the early hours of yesterday morning. Wind speeds of up to 180 mph were registered, the highest since records began.

Worst hit was the fishing village of Mousehole, the point at which the tornado hit land for the first time, shortly after midnight.

The sense of shock among inhabitants was palpable as the process of clearing up began. Initial estimates suggest that it could take as long as three years to restore the popular tourist resort to its former picturesque self.

"Cornwall has seen nothing like this since the great storm of 1775," said Leslie Abbott, the leader of the county council, whose planning department now has to oversee the village's revival. "The devastation is unbelievable. It's as though the place has been hit by a

Annotations:

- Strong headline
- Byline
- More passive verbs
- Technical details
- Less emotive or sensational language
- More complex words and sentences
- Longer paragraphs, with more than one sentence
- Quotations, perhaps from officials rather than members of the public

Redrafting

✔ Have you written in an appropriate style all the way through?

✔ Have you written in short paragraphs?

✔ Do you need to set out the report as though it was on a real newspaper page? (See the section on *Making a newspaper front page*, on page 63.)

✔ Can you add an image that works with the article?

(See the section on *Reading a newspaper report*, on page 22.)

Say "photo opportunity"

Making a newspaper front page

This section will help you to design and make a front page for a newspaper. It might be about an event from a story, or part of a media assignment. (See the section on Writing a newspaper report, *on page 59, and the section on* Reading a news report, *on page 22.)*

Can you turn over now?...
I've read the front page

Purpose and audience

The purpose and **audience** will depend on what type of newspaper it is. The two main types of newspaper are *tabloids* and *broadsheets*. This section will help you to create front pages for both types.

Tabloid newspapers (such as *The Sun* and *The Mirror*) usually present news in a brief and easily understood way, trying to make it appeal to as many people as possible. They will often feature plenty of pictures.

Broadsheet newspapers (such as *The Times* and *The Independent*) usually present the news in more detail, and have sections which comment on and analyse news events. In general, there will be fewer pictures and more words.

The purpose of the front page is to:

- ◆ grab the reader's attention (so that they buy the paper)
- ◆ make particular news items seem important
- ◆ start to tell the most important story, or stories
- ◆ make the reader think or feel in a particular way
- ◆ give the reader a sense of what else is inside the paper.

An example of a tabloid layout

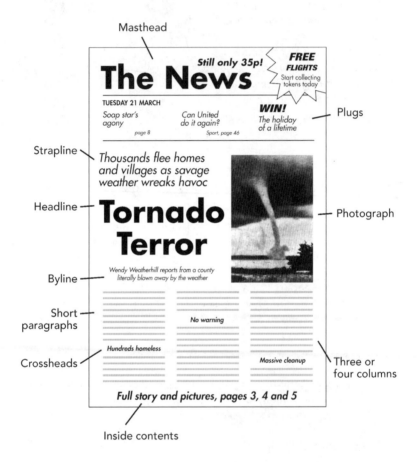

Masthead

The News

Still only 35p!

FREE FLIGHTS Start collecting tokens today

TUESDAY 21 MARCH

Soap star's agony page 8

Can United do it again? Sport, page 46

WIN! *The holiday of a lifetime*

Plugs

Strapline — *Thousands flee homes and villages as savage weather wreaks havoc*

Headline — **Tornado Terror**

Photograph

Byline — *Wendy Weatherhill reports from a county literally blown away by the weather*

Short paragraphs

No warning

Crossheads — *Hundreds homeless*

Massive cleanup

Three or four columns

Full story and pictures, pages 3, 4 and 5

Inside contents

An example of a broadsheet layout

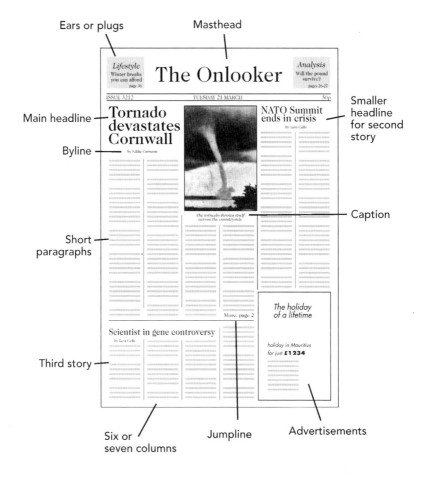

Ears or plugs

Masthead

Main headline

Byline

Short paragraphs

Third story

Six or seven columns

Jumpline

Advertisements

Smaller headline for second story

Caption

Lifestyle
Winter breaks you can afford
page 36

The Onlooker

Analysis
Will the pound survive?
pages 26-27

ISSUE 3212   TUESDAY 21 MARCH   50p

Tornado devastates Cornwall
by Eddie Currents

NATO Summit ends in crisis
by Levi Cells

The tornado throws itself across the countryside

More, page 2

The holiday of a lifetime

holiday in Mauritius for just **£1234**

Scientist in gene controversy
by Levi Cells

Redrafting

✔ Have you written in an appropriate style? (See the section on *Writing a newspaper report*, page 59.)

✔ For a tabloid front page, have you written in short paragraphs?

✔ Is the layout realistic? Does it have the right balance of words and images?

(See the section on *Reading a news report* on page 22.)

Getting the right balance of words and images was
proving difficult

Making a book cover

You might be making a new book cover for a text that you are reading. This section will help you to make it realistic and interesting.

Purpose

The cover will consist of a mixture of text, images and other design features. These work together to:

- grab the reader's attention
- draw the reader into the book
- give an idea of the **genre** (type) of book
- give clues about the story, characters and setting.

You will need to decide what you think is important or essential in the novel, and try to bring this out in the cover. In the example on the next page, what aspects of the story are being emphasised? What sort of **audience** is the story aimed at?

Audience

If you are making a cover for a novel, you need to think about what sort of reader the book is for. Obviously, a book for children will have a different cover from a book that is written for adults.

Writing

(See the example on pages 68 and 69.)

Redrafting the text

Think carefully about the writing on the back cover:

- ✔ Have you given away too much of the story?
- ✔ Does it need breaking into shorter paragraphs?
- ✔ Can you end it in a more intriguing way?

An example of a back cover

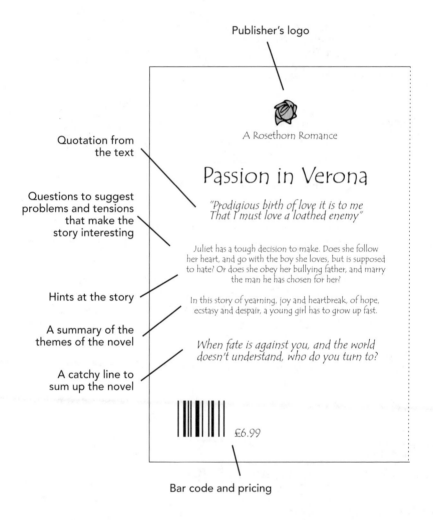

Publisher's logo

A Rosethorn Romance

Passion in Verona

"Prodigious birth of love it is to me
That I must love a loathed enemy"

Juliet has a tough decision to make. Does she follow
her heart, and go with the boy she loves, but is supposed
to hate? Or does she obey her bullying father, and marry
the man he has chosen for her?

In this story of yearning, joy and heartbreak, of hope,
ecstasy and despair, a young girl has to grow up fast.

When fate is against you, and the world
doesn't understand, who do you turn to?

£6.99

Quotation from
the text

Questions to suggest
problems and tensions
that make the
story interesting

Hints at the story

A summary of the
themes of the novel

A catchy line to
sum up the novel

Bar code and pricing

An example of a front cover

Spine

Strong image and striking design

The writer's name

A clear, bold title, in an appropriate style

Publisher's logo

Making a cartoon strip

In English, you might be turning a story, a poem or a scene from a play into a cartoon strip, showing your understanding of it. You might be using a cartoon strip as part of a leaflet – to tell younger students about bullying, for example. Or you might just be exploring this way of telling a story.

Purpose

A cartoon strip is a series of drawings telling a story. Like any other type of **text**, cartoon strips can have many purposes – to amuse, to inform, to entertain, and so on. Importantly, they tell a story using mainly pictures rather than words.

Audience

Cartoon strips are drawn and written for many different **audiences** – for children, in comics; for both children and adults, in newspapers; for older children and adults, in graphic novels. For older audiences, they might be more complicated, or have more serious subject matter. There may also be more words.

Comic strip conventions

Like all kinds of text, cartoon strips follow conventions or rules. For example, it is understood that the first of these images means 'a thought' and the second means 'speech'.

Some more of these conventions are labelled on the example on the next page. Try to use a variety of these in your own cartoon strip, so that you do not just draw a series of very similar pictures.

Title frame

Captions in boxes
to tell story

Establishing frame,
to set the scene

Sound
effects

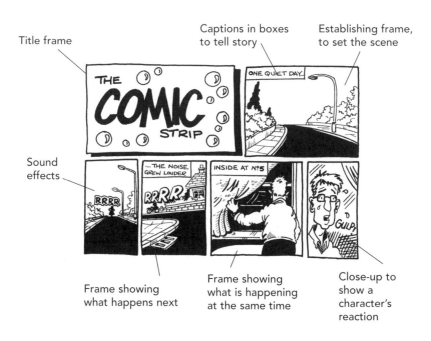

Frame showing
what happens next

Frame showing
what is happening
at the same time

Close-up to
show a
character's
reaction

Caption
to explain
where or
when

Thought bubble

Speech bubble

Reader sees over
character's
shoulder

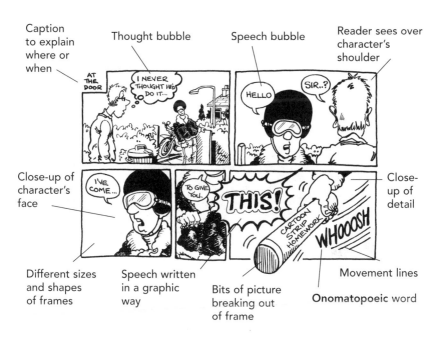

Close-up of
character's
face

Close-
up of
detail

Different sizes
and shapes
of frames

Speech written
in a graphic
way

Bits of picture
breaking out
of frame

Movement lines

Onomatopoeic word

It is a good idea to sketch your cartoon strip roughly, before redrafting it neatly.

If you are not confident about drawing, then it might help to look at how people and faces are drawn in other cartoon strips, and to copy them.

Redrafting

✔ Have you made the **narrative** (story) very clear?

✔ Have you used a variety of conventions, to keep it interesting?

✔ Could you add any more words – in captions, speech bubbles, or sound effects?

✔ Is there enough in the background in each frame? Is it cluttered?

✔ Could you add more colour?

Could you add more colour?

Making a storyboard

A storyboard is a series of sketches, used to plan a piece of a film or television programme. It shows camera shots and explains their effects, and gives an idea of the soundtrack, including sound effects and music.

Purpose

The purpose of a storyboard is to show what will be filmed. It is not a cartoon strip; it is more like a set of instructions for filming. The drawings do not have to be brilliant; they just have to give a clear idea of what the camera must show.

Your reason for storyboarding a sequence (piece of film) might also be to show your understanding of part of a story, and of how it might be told through film or video.

Audience

Technically, the **audience** for a storyboard are the people turning it into an actual film.

What to include in a storyboard

As well as pictures, you should include some technical instructions in your storyboard. For example:

Number 1

Cut suddenly (from black) to medium close-up from side, of girl pointing off screen. Fog in background.

She is positioned to the right, to create a sense that what she is pointing at is only just out of shot.

Distance of camera

Angle of camera

Other important details

Number 2

Fast dissolve to extreme close-up of girl's hand pointing into fog, to build horror and suspense, and to focus audience's attention on how she is shaking with fear.

Sound: screaming; music builds

How does one camera shot change to the next?

Main effects of shot

Sound effects and music

Number 3

Cut to point-of-view shot, showing the empty coffin as the girl sees it.

Camera zooms in quickly to close-up.

Sound: music pauses; girl whispers "No!"; music reaches climax.

Details of points of view

Details of camera movement

Camera shots

Vary the kinds of camera shots you use, to achieve different effects. Some different camera distances are:

Extreme close-up (ECU)

Close-up (CU)

Medium shot (MS)

Long shot (LS)

Some different camera angles are:

High angle

Low angle

Tilted frame

Side angle

Some other shots include:

Two shot

Over-the-shoulder shot

Point-of-view (PoV) shot (showing what a character sees)

Camera movement:

- zooming in or out (camera stays in one place, but the image gets bigger or smaller)
- tracking (whole camera moves along to follow action)
- panning left or right; up or down (camera stays in one place, but turns from side to side)
- tilting (camera stays in one place, but tilts up or down)
- circling (camera moves around the subject)

Pan left or right

Tilt up or down

◆ camera moves up and down.

Raise or lower

Some ways of changing from one shot to another include:
- ◆ cutting (straight from one shot another)
- ◆ dissolving (one shot turns gradually into another)
- ◆ wiping (one shot slides across another)
- ◆ fade to and from black (or white, or red...).

Some effects of shots are to:
- ◆ set the scene
- ◆ create atmosphere
- ◆ create tension or suspense
- ◆ show what a character is seeing (their point of view)
- ◆ show what a character is feeling or thinking
- ◆ show a character's reaction to something
- ◆ draw attention to one of several characters
- ◆ show the relationship between characters
- ◆ draw the audience's attention to a detail.

3 Drafting and Redrafting

The stages of writing

This section gives reminders about the different stages in producing a piece of formal, polished writing. Sometimes, you will not go through all these stages, because there will not be time, or it would not be appropriate – in a piece of journal writing, or an exam essay, for example.

Notemaking (see page 80)
- gathering ideas
- collecting useful words
- annotating texts
- brainstorming
- spider diagram or mind map.

Planning (see page 82)
- flow diagram of key points
- paragraph plan
- opening sentence.

Drafting (see page 83)
- turning ideas into sentences
- turning sentences into paragraphs
- experimenting.

Editing (see page 85)
- reading through, thinking about how effective the text is as a whole
- marking changes and corrections to make.

Redrafting (see page 85)
- making changes and corrections on a word processor or rewriting by hand, with changes and corrections
- producing the final draft.

Checking (see page 85)
- reading through carefully, correcting any mistakes.

Now all she had to do was to read through it caerphilly

Notemaking

There are many different ways of making notes and writers develop approaches that suit them best. However, it is essential to collect ideas and information before you begin a piece of writing.

"You need more ideas…"

◆ One way to do this is to make lists of points or key words. For example:

Animal experiments

vivisection = experiments on live animals

Unnecessary cruelty (see 2nd article)

Alternative research methods are available
(see 1st article)

"…most reliable way to research effects of
drugs is on something that is alive". (Quote
from 2nd article)

◆ 'Mind maps' can be an effective way of developing and sorting ideas. For example:

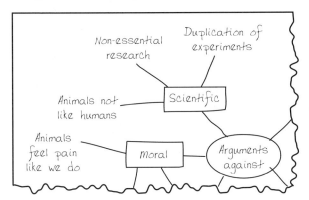

◆ Sometimes, your notes will be annotations (markings) on texts that you have read. For example, a poem that you are writing about, or an article that you are getting information from:

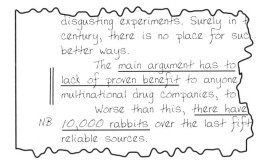

Planning

When you have collected your ideas together, make your plan.

This example is a plan for writing about both sides of an argument. It is a paragraph plan, and it also summarises the main points, which will be explored in detail:

For and against animal experiments

Introductory paragraph
"When you take a medicine, or use a cosmetic, do you know how it was tested? Well..." Why is it an important issue?
Facts about how much testing happens.

Arguments on each side
(include quotations, statistics and other evidence)

Against	For
Alternative research methods are available	Speeds up medical research
Unnecessary cruelty	Better that animals suffer than people
Animals and humans are so different that many results of this research are meaningless	The most reliable way to research effects of drugs is on something that is alive
Much of the testing is unnecessary (too many experiments)	Labs and experiments are controlled so that animals do not suffer unnecessarily
Lots of the research is for luxury items, such as cosmetics	People will use cosmetics, and it is essential that they are completely safe

Concluding paragraph
Summary – own thoughts

Drafting

This is the stage where you turn your ideas into sentences and paragraphs, experimenting to make your writing as effective as you can. This is an opportunity to explore and develop different ideas and to see where they go.

On a word processor, you can keep making changes to what you have written as you go along. On paper, you can mark changes on your draft. Sometimes you may need to redraft a paragraph more than once. For example:

It may help to write down some words and phrases before putting them into sentences

boy walking

dark

lonely

rustling leaves

winter evening

Try reading what you have written to yourself. Does it create the effect you want?

No atmosphere

The boy was walking in the
woods alone. It was getting
dark and the leaves were
rustling. Suddenly, there was a

The afternoon drew on
~~It was nearly four o'clock,~~
and the ∧ light was fading.
       thin December
       stumbled
The boy ~~was~~ alone in the
woods, ~~hurrying~~ through
   last Autumn's
~~the~~ rustling leaves.

Suddenly, there was a

Keep adding, taking out or changing words to give your writing more impact

The afternoon drew on, and
the thin December light was
fading fast. In the woods,
the boy stumbled alone
through <u>last</u> autumn's leaves.

Suddenly, there was a...

Add bit about
the memory and
getting home

Drafting is not just about adding on to the end of what you have written. You can keep going back and inserting more details to add to the effect

The afternoon drew on, and
the thin December light was
fading. In the woods, the boy
stumbled alone through last
autumn's leaves. However hard
he tried to put what he had
seen out of his mind, he
could not keep the memory
from returning. He had to get
home. Everything would be all
right when he was home.

Suddenly, there was a

Editing, redrafting and checking

Once you have written a rough draft, the next stage in the writing process is to read, check and mark changes on what you have written.

First, think about the content

Consider the following points:

- ✔ Does the piece of writing do what it is meant to do?
- ✔ Have you used language which is appropriate for your **audience**?
- ✔ Is the piece the right length?
- ✔ Is there anything which is not clear? Are any sentences difficult to follow?
- ✔ Is your writing organised in the most effective way? For example, are the paragraphs in the best order?
- ✔ Could any words or expressions be replaced by more effective ones?
- ✔ Should anything be added?
- ✔ Should anything be taken out?
- ✔ Could the beginning or the ending be improved?
- ✔ Think about the comments that have been made on your previous work: how might these help?
- ✔ Are there any targets that you have set yourself on previous writing that you should remember now?

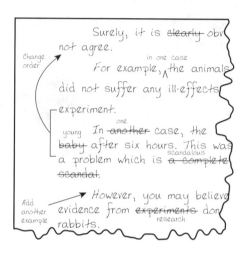

The handwritten draft reads:

Surely, it is ~~clearly~~ obv...
not agree.

Change order

For example, ^in one case the animals
did not suffer any ill-effects
experiment.

young In ~~another~~ one case, the
~~baby~~ after six hours. This was
a problem which is ~~a complete~~ scandalous
~~scandal.~~

Add another example

However, you may believe
evidence from ~~experiments~~ research don...
rabbits.

Next, think about the technical accuracy

Consider the following points:

- ✔ Are there any spelling mistakes? Have you used a dictionary or a spell-checker?
- ✔ Are the full stops and capitals in the right places?
- ✔ Is speech set out properly?
- ✔ Are there any other punctuation mistakes?
- ✔ Have you used paragraphs correctly? Do they begin and end in the best places?
- ✔ Think about the kinds of mistakes that have been corrected on your previous work. Check carefully for these.

Two bee shore she rand the
spiel cheque

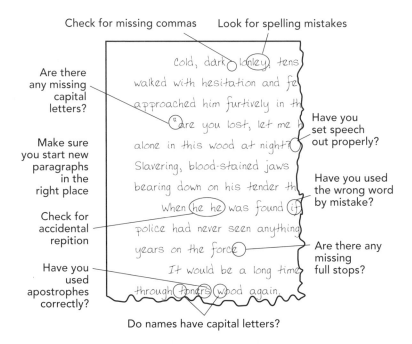

Check for missing commas   Look for spelling mistakes

Are there any missing capital letters?

Make sure you start new paragraphs in the right place

Check for accidental repition

Have you used apostrophes correctly?

Have you set speech out properly?

Have you used the wrong word by mistake?

Are there any missing full stops?

Do names have capital letters?

Cold, dark, lonley, tens
walked with hesitation and fe
approached him furtively in th
"Are you lost, let me
alone in this wood at night?
Slavering, blood-stained jaws
bearing down on his tender th
When he he was found (if
police had never seen anything
years on the force
It would be a long time
through toners wood again.

Final draft

The final draft is what you have been working towards; the version which contains all the changes and corrections that you have decided to make. Think carefully about presentation. If you are word processing, look at the advice on page 88.

Final checking

Read your writing through and check for any mistakes that remain.

Using a computer

You do not need a computer to produce excellent work, but if you use one, make good use of it to edit and develop your writing.

- When you word process something, you can edit it and redraft it very easily, so take advantage of this. Experiment by putting words, sentences and paragraphs in different orders. Try putting different words in and see what they look like; you can always delete them afterwards. Can you go back and add more in the middle?

- Always save your work, so that you can go back and edit it, and so that you can print it out again if you need to.

- Always use the spell-checker.

Make your work readable and well-presented

- Paragraphs can either be indented, or you can leave a line between each one, but *do not forget them*.

- Always leave a space after a piece of punctuation – a comma, or a full stop, or a question mark – before you write the next word.

- Always check your work very carefully for typing mistakes. The spell-checker will not find them all.

- Avoid using a font which is hard to read. *For example, this is quite hard to read, so you would only use it if you need to imitate handwriting.* This is good for a science fiction title, but terrible for anything else.

- If you are typing a long piece of work, don't use a font size which is very small and difficult to read.

- On the other hand, if you use a huge font size, it can look silly. Keep this for titles, or for particular effects.

4 Punctuation

These are simple reminders of some punctuation rules. They are meant to remind you of what you know, not to teach the rules from scratch.

Apostrophes

Apostrophes have two uses.

Firstly, they show that one or more letters are missing from a word (the apostrophe of *omission*). For example:

can not	→	can't
could have	→	could've
do not	→	don't
Here!	→	'ere!
It is	→	it's
must have	→	must've
of the clock	→	o'clock
should not	→	shouldn't
that is	→	that's
they are	→	they're
was not	→	wasn't
will not	→	won't
you are	→	you're

People say they feel left out when I'm around...

Secondly, they show that something belongs to someone or something else (the *possessive* apostrophe):

The dog's bone
The baby's pram
The cat's computer
The earwig's headache

The exception to the rule is 'Its', as in 'The dog lost its bone'.

In a plural the apostrophe goes after the 's':

The dogs' bones	The babies' prams
The cats' computer	The earwigs' headaches

Some other, tricky, plurals are:

children's	fishes'	women's
men's	people's	sheep's

Brackets

Brackets are used to insert a word, phrase or idea in the middle of a sentence. For example:

As the rain began to fall (more heavily than she could remember) Helen walked briskly along the busy street.

Brackets are also used to add a less important idea. For example:

There were two men in the bank at the time. (There was a child there, too, but she can't have been involved in the robbery.)

It's just that something
always comes between us...

Capital letters

Capital letters are used to separate sentences from each other. Every sentence starts with a capital letter and ends with a full stop (or a question mark, or an exclamation mark).

No... the capital of France is not F...

Capital letters are also used for:

- names
- days and months
- the main words in titles of texts
- initials
- the word 'I'

Joe, from Huntingdon

Tuesday, 4th June

Harry Potter and the Philosopher's Stone

J K Rowling

As the fire alarm went off, I walked quickly to the door.

Colons

I was just an ordinary full stop until things got on top of me...

Colons are used to introduce a list. For example:

In his pockets the police found several items: keys, coins, a wallet and a torn photograph of a young woman.

Colons are used to introduce an example or a quotation. For example:

The poet uses a metaphor to describe the dog: "...a snarling bomb, waiting to explode".

Colons are used to introduce a main idea. For example:

There is only one thing to remember: survival is essential.

91

Commas

Commas are used in two ways.

Firstly, they separate the items in a list. For example:

> In his pockets the police found keys, coins, a wallet and a torn photograph of a young woman.

Secondly, they separate parts of a sentence. For example:

Separating a phrase or clause at the start of a sentence

Separating a phrase or clause in the middle of a sentence

> After a terrible night's sleep, I got up at seven o'clock and left for work as usual.

> I waited at the bus stop outside my house, where I sheltered from the drizzling rain, then caught the bus for work.

> I arrived at the office after a journey of 40 minutes, wet and late.

Separating a phrase or clause at the end of a sentence

It's just a matter of comma-sense!

Paragraphs

It is difficult to give strict rules about where paragraphs should start and stop. However, it is useful to remember these guidelines.

You should start a new paragraph when:

- ◆ you change from one topic or point to another
- ◆ what you are writing changes from one time to another
- ◆ what you are writing changes from one place to another
- ◆ you change from one speaker to another, when writing out speech
- ◆ you would want a reader to pause for thought.

It is sometimes useful to look at a text like the one you are writing to see how the writer has used paragraphs.

If you are writing by hand, you should set new paragraphs in from the margin. If you are word processing, you can leave out a line instead.

So where d'ya want these paragraphs?

Semi-colons

Semi-colons are used to connect two related ideas in a sentence. For example:

Half of me wants to stop and half of me wants to carry on...

> The guards knew at once how the prisoner had escaped; there was a large hole in the wall.

> The hamster was gone; the cat looked very pleased with itself.

Sometimes semi-colons are used to connect two contrasting ideas, instead of the word 'but'. For example:

> She was brave; he was a coward.

Speech marks

Speech marks round each piece of speech

If the speech starts in the middle of a sentence, put a comma before it

> "Hi Mum! We're home!" shouted Tasneem, dropping her bags in the hallway.
> Mum shouted back, "Hello Taz!" She came down the stairs and her face dropped as she saw Joe standing behind Tasneem. "Oh," she added icily. "Hello Joe."

A new paragraph when there is a change of a speaker

At the end of speech, any punctuation always goes before the speech marks

Comma (or question mark, or exclamation mark) if the sentence continues

5 Presentations

A formal presentation needs careful preparation. As well as thinking through your ideas or points, you need to plan how you will present them effectively. This section will help you to do this.

Purpose

You must think carefully about what you are aiming to do in your presentation:

♦ Are you explaining ideas?
♦ Are you persuading your **audience** to think or feel something?
♦ Are you giving information?
♦ Are you telling a story?
♦ Are you giving a report?

Audience

How you present your ideas will depend on what your audience is like. For example:

♦ How big will your audience be?
♦ What age will they be?
♦ Will you know them well, or will they be unfamiliar?
♦ What will they know already? What will you have to explain?
♦ Will they expect you to be very formal, or not?
♦ Would it be appropriate to make jokes, or should you be serious?

Structure

You could work through the following steps:

Beginning
How will you begin? Do you need to explain what you are going to talk about? Can you get your audience's attention? For example, with a striking fact, a piece of strong description, a powerful feeling, something provocative, or something shocking?

Middle
How will you keep your audience interested? If you are explaining something, how can you break the information down into easily understandable points? What is the best order to put these points in? If you are trying to persuade your audience, how will you use evidence and examples? If you are reporting on something that you have done or seen, what do you need to include and what could you leave out?

Ending
How will you end in a way that leaves a strong impression on your audience? (Not just "That's it.") Can you sum up your main ideas? Could you end with a question? What do you want to leave your audience thinking about?

Visual aids

Visual aids can make a presentation easier to follow, because it gives the audience something to focus on. It is easier to talk about something that you are looking at. You might:

- show the audience objects or photographs
- make a handout
- write up key words or ideas, using pieces of paper, a flipchart, a whiteboard or blackboard, or a projector

- project images on an overhead projector
- use video extracts
- use computer presentation software.

Notes

Notes are very useful for prompting and reminding you as you speak. However, it is very important that you do not just read your presentation aloud. Notes need to be:

✔ brief
✔ clear
✔ easy to follow, when you are talking.

They might be:

- a list of headings for each part of the presentation, for example:

WORK EXPERIENCE

Introduction
Where? Why I chose this (future career)

First impressions
Smell. Terror. Rabbits.

- key words or phrases, for example:

Opening
You might think that infant schools are simple places to work. Well...

Responsibilities
reading - story corner - display work

...surprise of being treated more like an adult.

♦ quotations and statistics, that it would be hard to remember. For example:

37 children in class

Teacher works 70 hour week

Joe (aged 6): "I liked it best when the fire engines had to come, because of what Rosie did."

Presenting

When you are giving your presentation, it is essential to:

✔ make eye contact with your audience

✔ speak more slowly than you would normally

✔ speak loudly enough for everyone to hear clearly

✔ give the audience time to take in ideas, or to look at what you show them – do not race through your material

✔ be organised – it will help you to feel confident

✔ look prepared: do not refer to scrappy bits of paper; put your notes on cards, or a clipboard, for example.

Helpful phrases

Think about how you might use the following phrases in your presentation.

Explaining

First of all...
The next thing to...
If you... then...
You could... but...
It is important to remember...
An example of this is...
If you look closely at...
Finally...

Persuading

You might think that…

However,…

Firstly,…

For example,…

This photograph clearly shows…

Surely…

The evidence is that…

It's very clear that…

So, all this shows that…

Reporting (on something you have done, or seen, for example)

This picture was taken when…

Firstly,…

When we…

During the…

I had to…

When… I felt…

What I remember most clearly is…

Overall,…

Mummy'll come and see the lovely car you've painted in a minute…

6 Technical Terms

This chapter contains technical terms that will help you to understand how language and texts work. When they appear in the rest of the book, they are usually in bold type.

Accent

This is the way that people from particular places pronounce words.

*It is often important to people's sense of identity. However, there is still a lot of prejudice about accents. Look at how writers sometimes imitate accent in the way they write words down. What effect do you think this is meant to have? (See **Phonetic spelling** and **Received pronunciation**.)*

Adjective

An adjective is a word which describes a noun.

For example, "cold", "clever", "happy", "exciting"... .

Adverb

An adverb is a word which describes how something is done, and is usually put next to a **verb**.

For example, "quickly", "happily", "predictably", "softly"... .

Look, let me tell you how it's done

Allegory

An allegory is a story which can be read on more than one level. The characters and events in an allegory always represent something more general than just themselves.

For example, the novel Lord of the Flies *by William Golding, can be read just as a story about a group of boys on an island, or it can also be seen as a description of how people come into conflict with each other in the wider world. The animals in* Animal

Farm *by George Orwell, represent particular people in the political history of the Soviet Union. (See* **Fable***.)*

Alliteration

Alliteration is where words close to each other begin with the same letter. You will find it used quite often in newspaper headlines, in poetry, or in song lyrics.

When you find examples of alliteration, always think about its effects. Does it make the language more striking and easier to remember? ("Brown's Budget Beats Blues") Does it emphasise the rhythm of the words? ("Full fathom five thy father lies") Does it work like **Onomatopoeia***, imitating the sound of what it describes? ("Sudden successive flights of bullets streak the silence")*

Ambiguity

If something is ambiguous, then it could mean more than one thing, such as the newspaper headline "Giant Waves At Sea".

It might be possible to interpret a line or a word in a poem in more than one way. Sometimes this is deliberate. For example, "generous laughter" *could mean that the laughter is kind and giving, or that it there is lots of it. Sexual double entendre is an example of deliberate ambiguity. For example, in* The Duchess of Malfi *by John Webster, an intruder in the Duchess's bed chamber is described as having* "a pistol in his great codpiece".

Anecdote

An anecdote is a short retelling of an event, usually a personal experience. It is usually informal and often spoken.

Anthropomorphism

Anthropomorphism is when animals or objects are given human qualities or abilities, such as when animals in cartoons or children's stories talk, wear clothes, and behave like people.

In Animal Farm, *all of the animals are given human characteristics. They are able to speak, reason and organise themselves as humans do. Think about why writers use this device. What does it allow them to do? Look for examples of anthropomorphism in everyday life, in the way that people talk about animals, cars, belongings and so on. (See* **Personification**.)

Archaic

If language is archaic, then it is old-fashioned or not in use any more. For example, the word "perambulator" has been replaced by "pram".

Sometimes, modern writers will choose to use archaic language to create a particular association or feeling. How is the effect of the word "wireless" different from "radio"? To a modern reader, the language of older texts will often seem archaic:

> *"Thou tricksy Puck!*
> *With antic toys so funnily bestuck."*

Assertion

An assertion is a statement which is not backed up with facts or information.

For example, the statement "GCSE exams are obviously becoming easier" is an example of assertion. It is stated as

Last lesson you said that was 'assertion', now you say it's detention!

though it must be true, and does not allow the reader to disagree. Look for examples in **persuasive texts***, and think about why they are there. (See* **Opinion***.)*

Assonance

Assonance is where words close to each other contain the same vowel sounds.

For example: *"With dying light the silent fall of night."*

Does it make the language easier to remember? Does it help to create a mood or feeling through the repeated sounds? Does it work like **onomatopoeia***, imitating the sound of what it describes?*

Audience

The audience are the people who read a text or listen to what is being said: the people who buy a particular newspaper, for example.

When you are talking or writing about a **text***, think about the audience that it is intended for: Who are they? How is the form and language suitable for this audience? What does the writer assume about the audience? What does the text demand from the audience?*

When you are writing or speaking, you have to keep your audience in mind. Is the language and form that you have chosen appropriate? How do you want your audience to think, feel or react?

Ballad

A ballad is a poem or song, usually telling a story and usually passed on by word of mouth.

Most ballads follow a regular verse form, with a regular **rhythm** *and rhyme structure. The traditional song 'Young Waters' is a ballad, which has a typical verse structure. (See* **Metre***.)*

      o   /   o   /   o   /   o   /
   "His footmen they did run before

o / o / o /
His horsemen rode behind

o / o / o / o /
A mantle of the burning gold

o / o / o /
Did keep him from the wind."

Bathos

When a writer appears to be building up to something, then deliberately ends in an anticlimax, he/she is using bathos.

This is almost always comic, for example:

"Punark the Sorcerer was held in awe throughout the dark lands for his terrible powers of destruction, his unrivalled mastery of the ways of magic, his ferocious hatred for humankind, and his excellent recipe for lasagne."

Bullet points

- These are bulleted points.
- *They are used to make ideas clearer on the page, by separating them out, with a dot at the start of each one.*
- *Look at how they are used in* **informative** *and* **persuasive texts**, *where the ideas have to be as clear as possible.*

Clause

A clause is a distinct part of a **sentence**, which includes a verb.

Main clause

After she got home, Yasmin worked on her computer.

Subordinate clause

Cliché

A cliché is a saying or phrase that has been used so much that it has lost its effect. You should avoid these like the plague. They are a recipe for disaster.

Colloquialism

A colloquial expression is one that people use in everyday speech, but not in more formal writing.

*For example, "bloke" is a colloquial word for "man", and "getting stuck in" is a colloquial phrase for "starting". Look at how writers use them to create an informal **mood**, or to give a natural **voice** to a poem, for example. (See **Register** and **Slang**.)*

Conjunction

A conjunction is a word that links two parts of a **sentence**.

Examples include "as", "and", "because", "although", "Having…" and "but".

Consonants

These are the letters that are not vowels (see **Vowels**), like B, C, D and so on.

Couplet

A couplet is a pair of rhyming lines in a poem, such as the last two lines of Shakespeare's 18th Sonnet:

"So long as men can breathe or eyes can see,
So long lives this, and this gives life to thee."

*Think about the particular effect of rhyming couplets, especially at the ends of poems or **stanzas**.*

Dialect

People from different places or cultures often have different versions of the same language – with some different words, different expressions, and different ways of constructing sentences.

For example, in Yorkshire dialect, "frame thissen" means "get yourself organised". In Scotland, you might hear the sentence "That door is needing locked", which shows different sentence structure from Standard English.

Oral poetry (poetry which is passed on by word of mouth) will often be in dialect. For example, the ballad 'The Twa Corbies' is in Scots dialect, reflecting the speech of the place where it originated:

"As I was walking all alane
I heard twa corbies making a mane."

You should look for examples of how writers have used dialect forms and think about why they have done this.

(This is not the same as **Accent**. See **Standard English** and **Phonetic spelling**.)

Diction

In a text, diction refers to the kind of words a writer has chosen.

It can be useful to think about this if you are talking or writing about a text. You might write about how a writer has chosen a lot of **colloquial** words, or technical words, or words relating to nature, for example. If you wanted to say that there was a lot of old-fashioned language in a text, you might refer to the "**archaic** diction".

Discussion text

A discussion text is a text which presents all sides of an issue.

It often starts by explaining what the topic is, and then goes on to make points for and against. These points are backed up with evidence. It often ends with a conclusion, stating an **opinion** in favour of one particular side, or by asking the reader or listener to decide.

An example of a discussion text would be presenting arguments for and against school uniform, or for and against the use of animals when testing new medicines.

(See the section on Writing a discussion, page 32.)

Emotive language

Emotive language is language which is used to make a reader or listener feel a particular emotion.

Always think about the effects of emotive language. What emotions does the writer want to make the reader feel, and why? It is used a lot in **persuasive texts**, *such as*

He had not taken the rebuff easily…

advertisements, but also look for it in places where you might not expect it: in newspaper reports, for example. How does the headline "Jail This Beast Now" above a report of a murder trial suggest the reader should feel? (See **Persuasive language**.*)*

Explanation text

An explanation text is a text which explains a process or idea. It might be the answer to a question.

It often starts by describing what it is going to explain. This will usually be followed by a series of points, taking the reader or listener step by step through an idea or a process.

An example of an explanation would be a piece of writing on why language changes over time, or a talk about how to prepare for work experience. Pictures and diagrams might be important in an explanation text. (See the section on Writing to explain, *page 36.)*

Fact

A fact is something that can be proved to be true. (See **Opinion**.)

Fable

A fable is a story with a moral message.

Traditionally, fables have often been stories about animals, written or told to teach children about how to behave towards others, such as Aesop's fables. The novel Animal Farm *is a complicated* *fable written for adults, with a warning about the dangers of power. (See **Allegory**.)*

Foot

*See **Metre**.*

Genre

A genre is a "type" or "kind" of text. (In French, "genre" means "type".)

For example, in stories and films there are genres such as science fiction, horror, war, romance, comedy, and so on. Newspaper reports, magazine articles, leaflets and advertisements are all examples of non-literary genres.

It is important to think about what texts in a particular genre have in common. The features that they share are called the conventions of the genre. These conventions might include particular types of language, layout, or content. In a story or film, they might include typical settings, characters, events, themes, or ways that a story can develop.

Headline

A headline is the heading for a newspaper article.

Think about what effects it is meant to have on the reader.

Homonym

A homonym is a word with more than one meaning.

"Fire", "grass", "lead" and "case" are all examples of homonyms.

Homophone

Homophones are words that are spelt differently but which sound the same.

Examples include: "Sun" and "son", "led" and "lead"; "for", "four" and "fore"; "they're", "their" and "there".

They're not spelling errors, they're all homophones

Iambic pentameter

See **Metre**.

Icon

An icon is a kind of **symbol**. A graphic icon is a small picture.

You will find examples in leaflets, on computer screens and Web pages, in magazines and other texts. They make it easy for a reader to find their way quickly around a **text***.*

Imagery

Writers or speakers often create "pictures" which help the reader or listener to imagine something clearly.

For example, "as flat as a millpond" is an image to describe unusually calm waters. **Metaphor**, **personification** *and* **simile** *are types of imagery. Which of these does Wilfred Owen use in the line from 'Exposure':*
"the merciless iced east winds that knive us..."?

Imperative

An imperative verb tells the reader or listener to do something, like an instruction.

*"***Buy** *now!", "***Stay** *there!" and "***Check** *carefully" are all examples of imperatives. Look for how these are used in* **persuasive texts***.*

It is imperative that you go and fetch...

Information text

An information text is a text which gives the reader or listener information.

Examples include a bus timetable, a telephone directory, or a television guide.

*Often, an information text will also be an **explanation text**. An example would be a talk about fishing, which gives information about the sport, but might also explain what equipment you need or why people enjoy it.*

Instruction text

An instruction text is a text which tells the reader or listener how to do something. This will usually start by introducing the aims and what will be needed. It will go on to give a series of steps for the reader or listener to follow. Pictures and diagrams might be important in an instruction text.

Examples would include a recipe, or a guide to setting up a computer. An instruction text might be very simple – a road sign, for example. (See the section on Writing instructions, *page 40.)*

Layout

The layout is the way that words, pictures, graphics, paragraphs, lines of text, headings, subheadings and **symbols** are arranged on the page.

This can affect the way something is read and the effect it has. Look at this especially when you are writing about and comparing leaflets, articles or other informative and persuasive texts.

Logo

This is a graphic **icon** which identifies an organisation or company. You may find logos on products, advertisements or leaflets.

Metaphor

A metaphor is when something is described by saying it is something else.

That's one pound for the T-shirt and 27 for the logo...

When you are talking or writing about a metaphor, always think about its effect. For example, "A monster chewing at the beach" is a way of describing the frightening power and animal-like energy of the sea.

Think about the effect you can create with metaphors in your own writing, too. Look for examples of metaphors in everyday speech. Remember that a metaphor is different from a **simile**, because it says that something actually is something else, not that it is like something else.

An extended metaphor is where one metaphor leads on to others. For example, in the opening of Hard Times by Charles Dickens, Mr Gradgrind's forehead is described as a "wall". It then makes sense to describe his head as a "warehouse" and his eyes as "cellarage".

Metre

In poetry, the **syllables** in each line are sometimes stressed in a regular pattern. This is called metre.

To show this pattern, it can be useful to mark where the stresses fall, with slashes for stressed syllables, and circles for unstressed ones, like this:

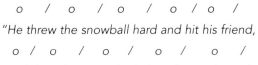

o / o / o / o / o /

"He threw the snowball hard and hit his friend,

o / o / o / o / o /

He did not know, or think, how fun might end."

Read this out loud a couple of times and listen to how the stresses in the lines emphasise particular words. Look for metre in poems, and look for how the rhythm can help to create a **tone** – cheery, or insistent, perhaps. Look for places where the rhythm suddenly changes: what is the effect?

Each pair of stressed and unstressed syllables is called a **foot**. An unstressed syllable followed by a stressed syllable (o /) is called an iamb. A stressed syllable followed by an unstressed syllable (/ o) is called a trochee. Different lengths of lines have different technical names. A line with five feet is called pentameter, one with four feet is called tetrameter, a line with three feet is called trimeter.

Two common types of metre, particularly in Shakespeare's verse, are **iambic pentameter** and **trochaic tetrameter**.

- Iambic pentameter has five iambic feet in each line, like the example on page 111.
- Trochaic tetrameter has four trochaic feet in each line, like this:

> / o / o / o / o
> "If we shadows have offended,
>
> / o / o / o / o
> Think but this, and all is mended"

*(See **Sonnet** and **Syllable**.)*

Microcosm

In a story, a microcosm is a miniature version of the world.

For example, you might describe a school as a microcosm of society, with its own rules, leaders, ways of doing things, and so on. In the novel Lord of the Flies, the island is a microcosm for the whole world: all the events and characters on the island represent aspects of the world as a whole.

It's a small world, isn't it?

Mood

This is the atmosphere or the feeling that a piece of writing creates.

A poem might have an ominous, sinister mood, or it might have a restless, yearning mood, for example. Look at how writers use language to create particular moods.

Myth

A myth is a story originally told to explain something, or to represent important truths.

For example, the story of the Garden of Eden can be read as the story of how all people are tempted into sin and lose innocence.

Narrative

Narrative is the way a story is told in any text.

*(See **Narrator** and **Structure**.)*

Narrative text

A narrative text is a text which re-tells events, often in the order in which they happened.

Examples would include a comic strip, an autobiography, a short story, or an episode of a soap opera. A written narrative will often contain words which put things in order, such as "first", "then", "next", "later", "meantime", "finally" or "while".

(See the section on Writing a short story, *page 48.)*

Narrator

The narrator is the person telling a story.

A first person narrative is where the narrator describes their own experience: "I walked into the room...". The narrator is then a part of the story, and might tell the reader what he or she is thinking and feeling. A third person narrative is where the narrator describes what other people do. "She walked into the room...". The narrator can be outside the story, and can be distanced from what is happening.

Noun

A noun is a word which names something.

This might be a person, place, object, feeling or idea. For example, "Paula", "London", "pen", "happiness", "education"....

Octave

*See **Sonnet**.*

Onomatopoeia

An onomatopoeic word is one which sounds like what it describes.

"Crash", "whisper", "rustle", "squelch", "bleat" and "snip" are examples of onomatopoeic words.

These are used by writers to create atmosphere, or to make an experience seem real. Think about how you can use onomatopoeia in your own writing, too. And know how to spell it.

With all the distractions of the classroom, she could barely hear the teacher's definition of 'onomatopoeia'

Opinion (implicit and explicit)

An opinion is something that one person believes, but which somebody else might not believe.

Explicit opinion is where somebody states their own view directly. For example, "I think young people are rude" is an explicit opinion. Implicit opinion is where the view is not stated directly, but it comes across anyway. For example, in "The young person was typically rude" the speaker's opinion of young people is implied by the word "typically". Look for these in **persuasive texts**, *and make sure that you can tell the difference between facts and opinions.*

Oxymoron

An oxymoron is a word or phrase that contains two contrasting ideas.

"Bittersweet" is an oxymoron. In Romeo and Juliet, *Romeo describes the confusions of being in love:*

"Feather of lead, bright smoke, cold fire, sick health."

As morons go, Oxy was pretty ugly

Pace

A piece of writing can seem to move quickly or slowly as it is read. This is known as its pace.

Look at how the pace of each of the sentences below is created by:

- *long or short sentences and words*
- *repetition*
- *punctuation*
- *mood*
- *alliteration*
- *long or short vowel sounds.*

  "Stretching lazily in the sunshine, listening to the soft, slow sounds of summer lingering on the heavy air, she drifted languidly into sleep."

  "Now. I have to move now. Quick! Quick! He's almost caught me! Running, almost tripping on the broken ground. Sharp stones under foot. Can't breathe, can't see! Where can I hide?"

Parody

If you parody a text, you make fun of it by imitating it and exaggerating its features.

Personification

Personification is where something inanimate (not alive) is written or spoken about as though it were alive.

For example, in Wilfred Owen's poem 'Exposure', the weather is treated as a living enemy: "Dawn masses in the east her melancholy army."

Sometimes an idea or a quality is turned into a character.

Madam is at death's door, she can't possibly see you now!

For example, you might decide that a character in a story is a "personification of goodness", or a "personification of bravery". In pictures, death is traditionally personified as a hooded figure with a scythe. In Animal Farm, each animal represents a particular aspect of human nature – greed, cunning, unthinking loyalty, and so on.

Persuasive language

Persuasive language is language that is meant to make people agree with a particular idea, or to make them feel something.

Emotive language is an example. You will find it especially in advertisements, newspaper articles and leaflets.

Even without language she could be pretty persuasive...

Persuasive text

A persuasive text is a text which aims to persuade the reader to think or feel in a particular way.

Examples would include a speech arguing for the banning of foxhunting, a leaflet protesting at the building of a new road, an advertisement, an election poster, or a trailer for a TV programme.

(See the section on Writing to persuade or to argue, *page 43.)*

Phonetic spelling

Phonetic spelling is a way of writing words to show how they are being spoken in a particular accent.

For example, in a novel the characters' speech might be written phonetically, as in this extract from The Mayor of Casterbridge *by Thomas Hardy:*

"But no – it cannet be! It cannet! I want to see the warrld!"

In a poem, a writer might use phonetic spelling to 'write' in their own accent. You need to consider why they have done this. (See **Accent** *and* **Dialect**.)

Plot

In a story or a novel, the plot is the order of events – what happens, and when.

Point of view/viewpoint

In a story, we will usually be aware of one character's thoughts and feelings more than others'. This is the viewpoint.

This may be the person telling the story, or it may be another character if the narrator tells us what they see, hear, feel and think. The viewpoint may change during the story. It is worth thinking about viewpoint in poems as well as stories. From whose point of view are we seeing what happens? Whose mind do we get inside?

Prefix

A prefix is attached to the beginning of a word, to change its meaning.

*For example, "***in****visible", "***un****fortunate", "***re****write" and "***dis****apply" are all words with prefixes.*

Pronoun

A pronoun is a word that can be used in place of a noun.

Examples are "I", "you", "she", "he", "they", "him", "her", "it", "them", "his", "their", "her", "its".

Pun

A pun (or **wordplay**) is a word that could have more than one meaning.

*It might be used in a poem: for example, in this **stanza** from 'London' by William Blake, the word "mark" means notice as well as a visible mark, drawing attention to both ideas:*

> "I wander thro' each charter'd street
> Near where the charter'd Thames does flow,
> And mark in every face I meet
> Marks of weakness, marks of woe."

In newspaper **headlines**, puns are often used to amuse and engage the reader. In Romeo and Juliet, Mercutio's dying speech is filled with puns:

> "Ask for me tomorrow and you will find me a grave man."

Received pronunciation

"RP" is an **accent** that is not associated with any particular place.

It used to be known as "BBC" or "Queen's English". Some people still have a prejudice that it is superior to regional accents.

Of course one is English!

Recount text

A recount text is a text which retells events, usually in the order in which they happened.

*Examples would include a diary or journal entry, an account of a science experiment, an **anecdote**, a news story or a witness statement in court. (See **Narrative text.**)*

Register

Register is how formal or informal written **text** or spoken communication is.

*For example, letters and conversations between friends will probably be in an informal register – chatty and full of **slang**. A school report, or a meeting between a parent and a teacher, will be in a more formal register. (See **Colloquialism**.)*

Report text

This is a text which describes what something is, or what it is like.

Examples would include an entry in an encyclopaedia, a travel guide book, a television reporter's description of a scene, or a piece of writing about the place you live.

Rhetorical question

Do you really need to be told what this is?

(It is a question which is supposed to have an obvious answer, and is being used to make a point. Look at how they are used in **persuasive texts***, to encourage the reader to think in the same way as the writer.)*

Experience had taught him that "Do I look fat in this?" was best treated as a rhetorical question

Rhythm

See **Metre***.*

Satire

Satire attacks powerful people or ideas, by being funny about them.

For example, comedians often make jokes about politicians. Many writers have attacked the powerful people or ideas of their times by making jokes at their expense. In Hard Times, Charles Dickens criticised nineteenth-century schools by making them seem absurd.

Sentence (See also clause):

- ◆ **Simple sentence** – A simple sentence has only one **clause**.

  This is an example. Look at where writers use them to make an idea direct and easy to follow.

- ◆ **Compound sentence** – A compound sentence is made up of two (or more) **simple sentences** joined by a **conjunction**.

  An example is, "The man did not move, because his feet were nailed to the floor."

- ◆ **Complex sentence** – A complex sentence is made up of a main clause and at least one subordinate clause.

  An example is, "Darren walked out of his house, looking around anxiously, and moved quickly over to his car."

Sestet

*See **Sonnet**.*

Sibilance

Sibilance is the repetition of "s" sounds in writing or speech to create a hissing effect.

In these lines from the play Hamlet, *Shakespeare uses sibilance to bring out Hamlet's disgust at his mother's behaviour:*

I'm afraid you've got sibilance...

> *"O, most wicked speed, to post*
> *With such dexterity to incestuous sheets!"*

Simile

A simile is when something is described by comparing it to something else. When you are writing about a simile, always think about its effect.

For example, "The crowd is like a swarm of wasps" describes how the crowd looks, sounds and moves. It also gives a feeling of danger. Think about the effect you can create with similes in your own writing, too.

*A simile is different from a **metaphor**, because it says that something is like something else, not that it is something else.*

IF IT'S LIKE A METAPHOR... IT'S A SIMILE!

Slang

Slang words are words used by a particular group, usually when they are talking informally.

For example, "bunking" is one slang word for truancy, and children in different places have lots of other words for it, too.

It is used in informal speech and writing, and is left out of formal speech and writing. Look at how writers use slang to suggest **mood** *or to create impact. (See* **Colloquialism** *and* **Register***.)*

Slogan

A slogan is a memorable phrase, used in advertisements or campaigns to make an idea stick in people's minds. The language is simple, and will often include **alliteration**, **wordplay**, **rhyme** or catchy **rhythm** to make them easy to remember.

Examples include "School dinners are winners!", "Don't drink and drive", or "YOUR COUNTRY NEEDS YOU!".

Sonnet

A sonnet is a particular form of poem, in which there are 14 lines, a regular **rhythm** and a regular rhyme scheme. Sonnets usually have two parts: an eight-line first section, called the **octave**, and a six-line final section, called the **sestet**. They are usually written in **iambic pentameter**.

The sonnet is a form that has been written for hundreds of years, and which is strongly associated with love poetry. The prologue to Romeo and Juliet *is a sonnet. (See* **Metre***.)*

Standard English

Standard English is a form of English that does not include **slang** or regional **dialect**.

It follows a set of conventions that some people call "correct" or "proper" English. You should avoid calling it these, as that suggests that there is something "wrong" with dialect or slang. Rather, standard English is "appropriate" in formal situations. Look for examples of where writers have not used standard English. Why have they done this? (See **Dialect**, **Register** *and* **Slang***.)*

Stanza

A stanza is a group of lines in a poem, usually following a regular and repeated pattern of **rhythm** and line length.

Stereotype

A stereotype is a view of a group of people, which sees them as all the same. This is usually unfair.

For example, an adult stereotype of teenagers might be that they are rude, aggressive, noisy and selfish.

The judging of 'Miss Stereotype' was not going to be easy...

A teenager's stereotype of adults might be that they all live boring, sad and conventional lives. You might find stereotypical descriptions in articles and adverts – of women, of old people or of the police, for example.

Structure

Structure is the way that a text is ordered or shaped.

*For example, it is how a story begins, develops and ends; it is the order of ideas in a leaflet; or it is the use of **stanzas** or verses in a poem. It is always useful to think about the structure when you are writing about a **text** of any sort.*

Suffix

A suffix is attached to the end of a word, to change its meaning.

*For example, "walk**ed**", "admir**able**", "strange**ly**" and "disappear**ing**" are all words with suffixes.*

Syllable

Syllables are the separate sounds that make up words. "Go" has one syllable. "Going" has two. "Inexplicable" has five.

*When writers use lots of one syllable (monosyllabic) words, this might help to create a hard, blunt or even angry **tone**, or a direct simplicity. When they use words with several syllables (polysyllabic), they can create a sense of sophistication, eloquence or technical complexity – like that.*

Symbol

A symbol is something that stands for something else.

*For example, on a persuasive leaflet, a picture of a candle might be a symbol of hope. In a piece of writing, a flying bird might be a symbol of freedom, or fire might come to symbolise aggression and conflict. A reader might find **symbolism** in something, even if the writer did not consciously mean it to be there.*

Symbolism

*(See **Symbol**.)*

Synonym

A synonym is a word that has almost the same meaning as another word.

For example, "hurry" and "rush" are synonyms. It can be interesting to work out what the difference is. For example, what is the difference between "dull" and "uninteresting", or "chase" and "pursue"? When would one be more appropriate than the other?

Text

A text is something that can be read. It could be a book, an image, a film, a **symbol**, a speech, a sign, or a piece of music, or anything else that has meaning for a reader or listener.

Sometimes, the word 'text' is used to refer only to words, rather than images or diagrams. Where there is a mixture of these – on a poster or on a Web page, for example – what is called the 'text' would usually be just the words.

Theme

This is an idea or topic which is important in a text.

For example, a story might be about the theme of loneliness, growing up, human nature, or friendship. You should be aware of what these are in any literary text, such as a poem, story, play or novel.

Tone

Tone is like mood. Just as you can speak in an angry or sad tone of voice, a text can have a tone.

*For example, a poem might be reflective or despairing; an advert might be lively or serious; a poster might be angry or accusing. This tone will mainly be created by the choice of words, but lots of other things create tone too – the length of **sentences**, **imagery** – even the **layout** and appearance of the page. (See **Voice**.)*

Trochaic tetrameter

*See **Metre**.*

Verb

A verb is a word which denotes an action, such as *"build"*, *"destroy"*, *"grow"*, *"think"*, *"say"*... .

Voice

Voice is a bit like **tone**. If you imagine the writer speaking a **text** to you, the voice is the tone you imagine them using – the personality behind the text.

Vowels

Vowels are the open sounding letters in the alphabet – A, E, I, O and U. There are other vowel sounds, like OO or OW. Y can also be used as a vowel in words such as "why" and "trying". (See **Assonance**.)

Wordplay

*See **Pun**.*